Exploring Ecology

49 Ready-to-Use Activities for Grades 4–8

Patricia A. Warren with Janet R. Galle

NSTApress

NATIONAL SCIENCE TEACHERS ASSOCIATION

Arlington, Virginia

Claire Reinburg, Director
Judy Cusick, Senior Editor
Andrew Cocke, Associate Editor
Betty Smith, Associate Editor
Robin Allan, Book Acquisitions Coordinator

ART AND DESIGN David A. Serota, Director
  Linda Olliver, Graphic Designer
PRINTING AND PRODUCTION Catherine Lorrain-Hale, Director
  Nguyet Tran, Assistant Production Manager
  Jack Parker, Electronic Prepress Technician

NATIONAL SCIENCE TEACHERS ASSOCIATION
Gerald F. Wheeler, Executive Director
David Beacom, Publisher

Library of Congress Cataloging-in-Publication Data

Warren, Patricia, 1939-
  Exploring ecology : 49 ready-to-use activities for grades 4-8 / by Patricia A. Warren and Janet R. Galle.
    p. cm.
  Includes bibliographical references.
  ISBN 0-87355-251-2
  1. Ecology—Study and teaching (Elementary) 2. Ecology—Study and teaching (Secondary) I. Galle, Janet. II.
Title.
  QH541.2.W295 2004
  372.35'7—dc22
                    2005003496

Featuring SciLinks® a way to connect, classroom ideas, and other materials are just a click away. Go to p. X to learn more about this resource.

Exploring Ecology

Contents

Section I: Management, Mechanics, and Miscellany

Section II: A Basic Introduction to Ecology

Section III: The Field Trip: Applying Ecology Concepts

Section IV: Integration and Extension

Foreword

The publication of a second edition is an indication of success of the first edition. *Exploring Ecology: 49 Ready-to-Use Activities for Grades 4–8*, this updating of *Ecology Discovery Activities Kit*, reflects curriculum for the 21st century—incorporation of the content standards of the National Research Council's National Science Education Standards (NSES) (NRC 1996). Specifically, *Exploring Ecology* addresses inquiry, life science, and science in personal and social perspectives standards for the K–4 and 5–8 levels of the NSES.

As noted in the foreword for the first edition, after the authors did several of the activities in their middle school in Brunswick, Maine, their school was the victim of arson. However, their former students had saved their field trip packets and the book started to emerge from the ashes. Students who experience *Exploring Ecology* will have greater potential to be productive decision makers in the 21st century. The following ancient Chinese proverb seems appropriate:

Plan for 1 year: Plant rice.

Plan for 20 years: Plant trees.

Plan for 100 years: Educate children.

Exploring Ecology will help you prepare students for the next 100 years.

Lloyd H. Barrow
Professor, Science Education
Southwestern Bell Science Education Center
University of Missouri–Columbia

About the Authors

Patricia A. Warren, B.S. Education, spent her entire career as a science educator in Maine schools. The last 33 of her 38 years in the profession were at Brunswick Junior High School in Brunswick, Maine, where she taught and was responsible for developing and implementing the science curriculum for grades six, seven, and eight. She has been active in both the Maine and National Science Teachers Associations, and has presented workshops for teachers at numerous conferences. She has served on local and state science curriculum committees, the Maine Educational Assessment Committee and was chairperson of the Autumn, 1988, National Science Teachers Association area conference in Portland, Maine. She served as the District 1 Director representing New England and the Maritime Provinces on the NSTA Board of Directors and was a member of the Executive Committee. From 1990 to 2000 she was field editor of *Science Scope*, the NSTA middle school journal.

Among the many awards she has received for excellence in the field of science education was the prestigious Presidential Award for Excellence in Science Teaching in 1996. Since retiring from the classroom in 1999, she lives most of the year in Florida. She revised the book for this second edition.

Janet R. Galle, M.S. Education, B.A. Speech, has 30 years of experience teaching preschool through college-level students in a variety of disciplines, including science, speech and language development, English, theater arts, and journalism. She has been chairman of a junior high science department, served as a member of the Board of Directors of the Maine Science Teachers Association, and has presented workshops at state and national science conventions. For nine years she was one of the journalism advisors at Mount Ararat High School in Topsham, Maine. She codirected nine musicals at Mount Ararat where she developed the performing arts program and currently teaches English. She has been a journalist for one of Maine's daily papers for 17 years. She and her husband live on a sheep farm in rural Maine.

About the Illustrators

Linda Olliver, former art director of NSTA, worked with the original sketches of Arek W. Galle, who was a student at the University of Rhode Island when he illustrated the first edition of this book.

SciLinks

How can you and your students avoid searching hundreds of science websites to locate the best sources of information on a given topic? SciLinks, created and maintained by the National Science Teachers Association (NSTA), has the answer.

In a SciLinked text, such as this one, you'll find a logo and keyword near a concept your class is studying, a URL (*www.scilinks.org*), and a keyword code. Simply go to the SciLinks website, type in the code, and receive an annotated listing of as many as 15 web pages—all of which have gone through an extensive review process conducted by a team of science educators. SciLinks is your best source of pertinent, trustworthy internet links on subjects from astronomy to zoology.

About This Resource

Exploring Ecology gives you a unique collection of 49 high-interest, hands-on activities for students in grades 4 through 8. These activities will make it easy for you to teach important ecology concepts and the science-as-inquiry skills recommended by the National Science Education Standards (NRC 1996). Designed for flexible use, the book allows you to choose from a wide range of activities for the classroom and the field. It works equally well as a resource for a sequential, eight-week unit on ecology as for a group of shorter, one- or two-week units.

By using the "Planning Guide" on p. 7 you can choose activities to plan and develop an ecology program unique to your Science program, supplement an existing environmental curriculum, or enhance a program for academically talented students. We found it extremely important to follow a plan that would, in the end, permit students to use the inquiry skills they had learned on our planned field trip that was the culmination for the unit.

The activities designated in sections II and III were very much teacher-directed. We never dismissed a class without reviewing what we had done that day and linking it to the other concepts that we had covered. We never intended nor do we recommend that teachers use all the activities. We carefully selected those we knew students would have to be able to use again on the field trip. We went very slowly and made sure students understood a particular concept and the skill that matched it. Whether it was identifying and counting populations, constructing a food web, or measuring temperature, they were able to link one skill to another.

Some of the activities were easier for our students because we already had some parts of the program in place. Early in the year we spend time learning to identify and classify local plants. Students did remember plant names and were able to use the information again. Other parts of our program incorporated some of the techniques we used previously so that it was not the first time students had used them. They were very familiar with some of the tools that they now encountered again.

However you use it, you'll find *Exploring Ecology* contains all the features a busy teacher needs. The book includes comprehensive teacher instructions, student worksheets that can be reproduced as often as necessary, and answer keys as appropriate. Each activity has been classroom-tested, and the helpful tips we've included will be beneficial to you.

Organization

We've divided *Exploring Ecology* into four sections. The activities are identified on p. XVI with a key that will tell you which are classroom-based, which are field activities, which duplicate a concept that has already been presented, and those that are extensions to other areas of the curriculum such as language arts, art, social studies, and science. Be sure to become familiar with Section I, "Management, Mechanics, and Miscellany," before you begin teaching the activities. It contains information that will help you organize necessary materials, prepare your classroom, and manage student activity in the classroom as well as in the field. A wide variety of approaches introduces important ecology concepts and allows students to practice the important skills of the scientific process: observing, classifying, communicating, measuring, predicting, inferring, hypothesizing, experimenting, collecting and analyzing data, drawing conclusions, and making generalizations.

Section II contains 35 activities that introduce the concepts of ecology, populations, communities, and food web/energy flow.

Section III contains much useful information to help you organize a successful trip. All of the material in this section will help you plan and carry out the event. Site selection, equipment needs, chaperones, discipline, and an activity schedule are clearly described.

The work in Section IV integrates ecology with language arts, social studies, and art and contains activities that extend the scientific approach. Some of these became Saturday Science programs. Others were used on the field trip and then incorporated into class events in language arts and art programs.

The National Science Education Standards that apply to the activities are listed at the beginning of each part of Section II. Pertinent excerpts from the book, *National Science Education Standards*, accompany some of the activities. The text of the book is available at *www.nap.edu/ books/0309053269/html/index.html*

Why Should We Teach Ecology?

Most communities today are affected by some ecological risk, whether it be hazardous waste, a dwindling supply of potable water, loss of farm or wetlands, increasing air pollution, or global warming. As a global community we face problems of overpopulation, desertification, acid rain, ocean pollution, ozone layer depletion, and the possibility of climate changes. Our students will someday be making decisions about these issues. The well-being of our planet depends on educated citizens with the wisdom to manage its resources.

Including ecology in our science programs gives us a wonderful opportunity to integrate the National Science Education Standards, "Science in Personal and Social Perspectives" Standards, into our programs. Such content Standards as populations, resources, and environments; natural hazards; and risks and benefits can be addressed with our students.

Teaching ecology also has some very immediate, short-term advantages. No matter where students live—city, country, or suburb—they can easily apply the concepts learned in this book to their own communities in very concrete ways. The hands-on nature of the activities guarantees students' interest and comprehension as they learn to think critically and logically, ask questions, and communicate the results of their research. The intense use of science-as-inquiry skills will continue to apply to all the sciences they will encounter in future science programs. We believe that ecology is a vitally important science. We also believe, based on our experiences teaching, that it's fun for both students and teachers. We hope you'll use this book of activities to discover the excitement of ecology for yourself.

Pat Warren
Janet Galle

Acknowledgments

Our biggest debt in producing this book is to our students. Without their enthusiasm and honest, constructive criticism, we would not have persevered. The sixth-grade teachers in other disciplines at our middle school hopped on the bandwagon and said, "We'll all go on the field trip!" They willingly planned with us, waded through mud flats, swatted black flies, and incorporated poetry, mapping skills, and artwork into their own classrooms.

Seventh graders returned to our classroom the following year as student aides; they collated field trip packets, counted mosquitoes with sixth graders who needed help, and ran every errand we asked. Jillian Galle stacked cans, piled meter sticks, sorted field guides, and stayed with the two of us until we were ready to quit.

Our high school advanced placement biology students added a new dimension as they gave up their study halls and ran to the middle school to act as peer tutors to our classes. The school librarians augmented our classroom resources. Parents helped by becoming teachers themselves on the field trip. The local newspaper staff covered our activities. Our administration and the secretaries supported us and took over some of our students who simply could not follow our rules. Our families never complained (at least not often) about our weird schedule.

Particular thanks for the first edition must go to Jean St. John who was our secretary and chief organizer, to the custodians who continued to tell us jokes and clean up after us, and to the staff of Curtis Memorial Library who responded to our every need.

Without the efforts and artistic skills of Arek Galle, who had to rework his drawings for the first edition as our whims changed from day to day, this book would not have been complete. To Dr. Lloyd H. Barrow we owe a debt of gratitude for his careful, accurate, scientific instruction and his belief in us.

Introduction to Science as Inquiry

Most students who graduate from our schools will not become scientists. Rather, they will be entering an increasingly technological world made more complicated by ethical, moral, and futuristic decisions forced upon them by scientific advances. Our young people need to become adults who will know how to explore problems, think through possible solutions, and make wise decisions. Science will play an extremely important part in their lives.

The National Science Education Standards (NSES) (NRC 1996) have created a mandate to us as teachers of elementary and middle school children to nurture and encourage intellectual curiosity, problem solving, and a commitment to learning. The students who leave us must not be alienated by dull science, but instead must have a sense of revitalization as they approach high school science and its various offerings.

To accomplish this task, elementary and middle school science must be a living, breathing, active subject. The controversy over approaches to teaching science must be secondary to the actual teaching of the subject. Whatever technical approach is used in a classroom, an infectious enthusiasm for the wonders of this world will be a teacher's best ally in teaching science.

This book places an emphasis on an inquiry approach to science education. No matter how primitive or unsophisticated hands-on activities are, the impact on young students is unequaled. Science is better understood when it is experienced. As a teacher, you do not need a mastery of the subject, but you do need flexibility, confidence, humor, and the willingness to make a few mistakes.

Science process skills are part of a basic, general curriculum and span all disciplines, paying dividends to the teacher who uses a process approach as part of the daily science program. The National Science Teachers Association recommends that 40 percent to 60 percent of science class time should be devoted to students' participation in discovery and exploratory activities. Students must find answers and questions for themselves. You can provide the guidance and the content they need to know. At that point a student's natural curiosity takes over.

Using an inquiry approach in the middle-level classroom can sometimes present problems, but here are a few guidelines to keep in mind.

- Most important for the novice is to have faith in the children. You may not know all the answers, but searching for them together is a learning experience more valuable than a given piece of information.
- Your attitude will be more important for your students' learning than any number of facts you require them to know. Enjoy the wonders of the natural world together.
- Using science processes requires the use of all senses. Encourage your students to look, feel, smell, listen, and, on occasion, taste.
- Firm rules for behavior when the class is working together must be established before activities get under way.

Timing of activities is of major importance. There must be enough work so students do not have time on their hands, especially when they are outside. Make sure you and your students understand the directions and that students know what is expected of them. Specific instructions are included with each activity to help make your teaching task easier.

The planning guide on p. 7 provides an overview of the entire program. The NSES recommend that teachers of science select science content and adapt and design curricula to meet the interests and experience of students. For middle-level students to conduct an extensive community field study, the abilities necessary to do the science must be presented in a sequential manner, and we have presented them that way.

In a chart on page XVI, the activities that teach a field skill in the classroom are designated by an "I" (for introductory). Those identified with a "D" (for duplicate) are supplementary and are generally used to reinforce those skills or concepts that the teacher feels have not yet been achieved. In some instances it was necessary to use a classroom model to take the place of an outside activity due to poor weather conditions. Field activities are identified with an "F" (for field).

Those activities that represent an effort to allow science teachers and other teachers to work together within and across disciplines are designated with an "E" (for extension) in the chart on p. XVI. The specific areas addressed are creative writing, art, social studies, and extended science activities. To continue to capture the enthusiasm generated by this classroom study we hosted Saturday Science to provide the extra time to create projects such as terraria and collages.

There are many more lessons and activities provided than can be used in a single teaching unit. It is of vital importance that you carefully plan a program that meets the needs of local curriculum objectives.

Activity Designations

To help in planning what you want to cover, the letters below designate four types of activities.

I   Introductory activity, classroom based
F   Field activity
D   Duplicate of a concept already presented
E   Extension

Section II, Part 1 Ecology	
Symbol	Activity
I	1
I	2
E	3
I	4
E	5
D	6
D	7
I	8
D	9

Section II, Part 3 Communities	
Symbol	Activity
I	15
I	16
D, E	17
F	18
E	19
I	20
F	21
F	22
I	23
F	24
F	25
F	26
I	27

Section II, Part 4 Food Web and Energy Flow	
Symbol	Activity
I	28
I	29
D	30
E	31
I	32
I	33
I	34
E	35

Section II, Part 2 Populations	
Symbol	Activity
I	10
F	11
I	12
E	13
I	14

National Science Teachers Association

SECTION I

Management,
Mechanics,
and Miscellany

Overview

Encouraging students to produce effective results with unfamiliar activities requires strong motivational techniques. Some that we will discuss here include putting up special bulletin boards, arranging the classroom around the study of ecology, using peer leaders and older students, and discipline.

To organize the students, activities, and equipment for this program, you must pay particular attention to details. We've put together this section to help you.

The outdoor classroom is an ideal place to enjoy learning. To take advantage of this setting, you and your students must be sure behavior is appropriate. Students who are well-prepared with clear goals assume responsibility for their own behavior, and in this section we will show you how to prepare easily and effectively.

Room Preparation and Bulletin Boards

Teaching ecology does not require special facilities, but it does require flexibility and some space. To prepare for this unit, it is wise to follow a few careful steps.

Room

1. Clean up the classroom, and get rid of old projects and other activities that are no longer necessary.
2. Clear off bulletin boards. These should now be used as direct teaching tools.
3. Organize equipment. Before this unit begins, collect gallon plastic milk jugs and a variety of 1- and 2-liter soft drink bottles. Line transects need to be made: See Activity 20 for explanation.
4. Visit your local chamber of commerce and beg for cast-off or outdated maps of your community. (You will need about one for every two students.)
5. Organize your field guides. They are frequently more helpful than textbooks. A suggested list is given in the bibliography on p. 245. What is available in your room? Can you buy field guides or include them in next year's budget? Go to the library and check out field guides you do not have. Ask students to bring in their own field guides when possible.
6. Arranging your room in groupings of desks or tables may be helpful. Students will generally be working in small groups for much of this unit.
7. Arrange for storage space. You will also need room for students to keep their equipment and other items. If you include Activity 35 (recycling), you will need a closet to store the bags.
8. Look over the list of materials and equipment. Plan ahead for what you will need.

Bulletin Boards

Before you begin this unit, start gathering old natural history and wildlife magazines. A plea to your students or the local library will generally produce back copies that someone is happy to get rid of.

Cut up the magazines for bulletin boards that will illustrate the major subjects of this unit. Cover one section with pictures of *populations* (include things like 50 seals on a beach, a lawn full of blades of grass, a single oak tree, humans on the street of a city). Label the pictures and include a definition of population.

Do the same for *communities* (include pictures like a rain forest, a pond, a fencerow, a rotten log, a giant cactus). Frequently, nature magazines will have a feature article on a "community." Again, label the pictures and include a definition of community.

Plan another bulletin board that will illustrate *energy flow*. This can be a food web of your own design, or you may wish to have students do this later in the unit. (See Activity 29.) Label the pictures, and provide a definition pointing out the interrelationships of all biotic and abiotic factors. You may include examples of the oxygen, nitrogen, carbon, and water cycles here.

Set aside a bulletin board for students to use. (See especially Activity 10.)

Materials and Equipment

The teacher instructions for each activity include a careful listing of the materials you will need to complete that particular activity. Included on this page and the next is a comprehensive listing of all materials and equipment used in these 49 activities. You will find many occasions on which you can substitute one item for another or invent a new item yourself, but this list will assist you in planning. Amounts will usually depend on the size of your class and on available funds.

- Lots of big white paper (newsprint is fine and frequently available from a local newspaper office or recycling center)
- Construction paper, all colors and white
- Magic markers, crayons, pencils, colored pencils
- Scissors
- Glue
- Clay
- Masking tape
- Rulers
- Meter sticks (at least 2 or 3 for each group)
- String
- Wood and large nails for the making of line transects
- Discarded nature and wildlife magazines
- Local and state newspapers
- Recent news magazines
- Blank transparencies (if you use an overhead projector in teaching)
- Gallon milk jugs, clean (at least 2 or 3 for each group)
- Large coffee cans
- Binoculars (nice to have)
- Soil thermometers or small alcohol thermometers
- Whistle
- Ziplock plastic bags
- Large plastic garbage bags
- Brown paper grocery bags
- Surveyors tape
- Trowels
- A standard scale
- Yarn—5 balls, yellow, red, green, black, and brown
- Dictionaries
- Atlas and world, state, and local maps
- Topographic maps
- Textbooks (with an ecology section) for limited reading
- Trade books (ask your librarian to provide you with a list of books on ecology)
- Field guides, suggested list in Bibliography

- Video, DVD, and websites, suggested list in Bibliography
- Music selections, suggested within the activities
- CD player
- Overhead projector
- Styrofoam or plastic cups
- Soil samples
- Timing devices (student watches will work)
- Hand lenses (many)
- Containers for plants
- Seeds
- Standard measure for water
- Large aquarium-like container with screen cover
- Gravel
- Charcoal
- Humus or rich soil
- Grass seed
- Crickets
- Chameleons
- Soil from the forest floor
- Funnels
- Large jars
- Rubbing alcohol
- Screening
- Paper towels
- White saucers
- Heat lamp
- Gallon glass jug
- Yeast
- Bromthymol blue
- Test tubes and test tube rack
- Eye droppers
- Liquid soap
- Salt

Planning Guide

The following 35 activities of Section I and the application activities of Section II constitute an eight-week unit for the study of ecology. The table below outlines one suggested use of the activities in this curriculum.

Whatever activities you use, you will need to select those that suit your program best, because you will not have enough time in eight weeks to use all 35 activities.

WEEK	MONDAY	TUESDAY	WEDNESDAY	THURSDAY	FRIDAY
1	Introductory Act. 1 At Issue Act. 2 Interview Act. 35 Recycle	Act. 3 Sensory Act. 7 Survival Act. 4, 5, 6 Definitions		Act. 9 Pond, Forest, Meadow Parts of the environment	
2	Begin Populations Population activities 10, 11, 12, 13, 14				
3	Act. 15 Mapping a Community Begin community activities 16, 17, 18, 19				
4	Act. 20 Demo Line Transect		Act. 21 Line Transect		
5	Act. 22, 23, 24, 25, 26, 27 Soils–Temperature				
6	Act. 28 Energy pyramid		Act. 29, 30, 31 Food Webs/Food Chains		
7	Act. 32, 33, 34, 35 Mother Nature's Recycling Projects		Prepare for Field Trip Section III		Field Trip Day
8	Synthesizing and Analyzing Data (Section III)				

Discipline

A Model for Positive Behavior in the Outdoor Classroom

Student behavior or misbehavior is the major deterrent teachers cite as the reason for not having their classes use the outdoor laboratory. The merit system described here has a twofold purpose.

- It states clearly to students the consequences of not following through with assigned tasks.
- It provides an inside alternative to the fieldwork for the teacher to use as a response to inappropriate student behavior.

Be prepared to use the indoor response if you must. One such occasion is often all that is needed for students to know you mean business. The model assumes that enthusiasm for the outdoor work will help students monitor their own behaviors.

Setting Up the System

The plan for positive student behavior in the outdoors is a simple point system. At the start of this unit, carefully discuss with students the behaviors they think will cause a negative reaction from the teacher toward the student. List these behaviors on the board. Possible responses might include fooling around, not doing homework, not paying attention in class, and running around outside.

After giving students a brief explanation of the culminating field trip, tell your students they must earn the right to participate in the field trip by accumulating merit points. Explain that you will assign each student five merit points per day and then will assume each student is a good student and has those points at the beginning of each day. The student's job is to simply keep the points, which assures the student a place on the field trip. You will make the decisions on point deductions, and you will not restore points.

Keeping Track of Points

On your class list, include the date of each class meeting. Record only points lost for misbehavior. Most students will end the unit with the maximum point total. You can write the names of students who lose points on the board to encourage attention to behavior.

Assigning Points for Infractions

The teacher determines the appropriateness of student behavior. Minor infractions are one-point deductions. They might include such things as forgetting homework, not paying attention, teasing other students, or not following instructions when working outside the school building.

Repeated problems with the same student or combinations of minor problems would lead to two- or three-point deductions.

Major challenges to the rules, of course, result in major point loss. Being sent out of class for improper behavior, fighting, destruction of equipment, or being sent back to the classroom when working outside are major problems. These would result in a five-point deduction.

Your determination of the point limit exclusion from Field Trip Day should not be unrealistic. If prefield trip work is three weeks long, the merit point total would be 75 points, 25 points for each five-day week. A point loss of 8 to 12 points should be consideration for exclusion. Fifteen points would definitely result in a student's staying at school instead of attending the field trip. The goal is to have all students understand clearly the importance of controlled behavior when a class is outside.

Alternative Assignments

Before the field trip, prepare an alternative assignment to replace the field assignment for those students who will not be allowed to go. A textbook chapter with questions to answer is an easily readied assignment, albeit not too exciting. Or you could assign work in trade books that parallel the subject matter. You must make sure that the student completes the inside work assigned.

Alternative Placement

If you must send a student inside, you must have a place to put him or her. Check ahead of time with another teacher for possible coverage. Perhaps you can assign a student a seat in the library.

Tips for Positive Behavior

- Specific assignments with clear objectives
- Fairness in assessing penalty points
- Insisting that each student assumes the responsibility for his or her own behavior

High School and Peer Leadership

A well-organized program of peer leadership provides support to the teacher in this active ecology curriculum.

Leaders From the Same School

One suggested peer leader program could involve the following:

1. Students one grade ahead of your class's level could request to be science aides during a free period.
2. Accept only students who have completed science in your class and are highly motivated, responsible individuals. (High grades are not necessarily a factor.)
3. Student aides can do a variety of jobs during the school year, such as stapling and collating papers, taking inventory, assisting students with research or experimentation activities, cleaning, gathering and sorting equipment, caring for classroom animals, running errands, tending bulletin boards, or experimenting on their own.
4. As Field Trip Day approaches, select a few of the most dependable students and ask if they can arrange their school schedules to accompany your class. Remember, they should have completed the program themselves the year before.
5. These select students may then be assigned to a group, working with the group on the line transect survey during the three weeks before the field trip. This gives all students involved a chance to develop a working relationship. This is an especially good move if your class has students with learning difficulties.
6. Peer helpers will frequently offer to help after school in preparation for the field trip.
7. On the day of the field trip, besides assisting a group, peer leaders make wonderful errand runners, thanks to their familiarity with the program.

High School Leaders

1. Contact the teachers of an advanced biology course at your local high school. Their students are usually seniors who may need community service credit. Be sure you receive permission from the high school principal as well as your own principal.
2. Ask for the opportunity to speak with the class to request their assistance with teaching the ecology unit. (Otherwise, you would need to meet with the high school teacher to explain the program.)
3. Explain to the students (briefly) the ecology program. Emphasize the benefits of older students working with younger students, both in terms of modeling behavior for younger students and the teaching opportunities provided to the older students.
4. The ideal program would allow a high school student to come once a week to a class. This would necessitate some coordination with the high school scheduling.
5. High school students can be assigned to "site" groups within your class and can work with those groups the weeks prior to the field trip, again establishing teaching relationships.

6. On Field Trip Day, each high school student can accompany his or her assigned group.
7. One of the high school student's assignments on Field Trip Day can be to teach a minicourse on any item of interest to the students. The subject could be something he or she is studying in biology, for instance, observing microscopic pond life, nematodes in the soil, or a lesson in ornithology. The point is to expose your students to something totally new.
8. Provide copying service for any papers the high school students may need for this lesson.
9. At the end of the unit, write a note (or send a balloon) to each high school student thanking each individually for the assistance.

Suggested high school student evaluation form, to be returned to their biology teachers

Student name	Overall enthusiasm	Field trip work	Minicourse prepared	In-class work with groups	Attendance	Comments	1–unacceptable 2–poor 3–average 4–good 5–excellent

Rank students 1 to 5 (5 highest score) in each category.

Health and Safety in the Field

Students With Health Problems

Before you begin using this book, contact the school health office so you know of any students who have health problems. You may have students with allergies to certain plants or insect stings. Know the appropriate action to be taken if a reaction occurs. The student may need to rest, avoid a certain area, or receive medical attention.

When you are in the field, have all medications on hand. Assign a student with a particular problem to an area that will not trigger allergic reactions. For instance, a student with a pine pollen allergy could be assigned to the ocean. When you are away from the school grounds, provide a health section of the permission slip to identify students with health problems for chaperones and other teachers.

Assign students with special needs to the areas most easily accessible. A student who uses a wheelchair should be able to work in the field. Identify the activities that students with special needs can perform, and monitor their progress. If possible, the parent of a special needs student could accompany that group and provide support for the students. Alternatively, working with special needs students is an excellent assignment for peer leaders or high school volunteers.

Some students fall under the Individuals With Disabilities Education Act and have an aide for class. The aide should accompany the student during all field experiences.

First Aid

Provide each group on the field trip with basic first aid supplies either in a kit or some other container. Include the emergency medical service telephone number. Also, include equipment necessary for your particular area of the country. It is wise to take a vehicle and a cell phone to each site in case of injury or emergency.

Addressing Individual Student Needs

When planning the lessons you will use to teach this ecology unit, you should include activities that can be accomplished by all students assigned to your science classes. Individual adaptations to learning based on individual education plans (IEP) need to be accommodated. Because most of the book's activities are for groups, you can carefully select assignments that capture the strength of each student.

Read "Health and Safety in the Field," p. 12, for suggestions on accommodating special needs students on field trips.

Working closely with special educators to make sure students clearly understand directions and behavioral expectations is extremely important. Rapid response to breaches of rules is also important. We had few behavior problems, and students were especially careful not to lose points that would prevent them from participating in the activities.

Science Process Skills

According to the *National Science Education Standards* (NRC 1996), there are several process skills that are a very important part of science for elementary and middle grade students. The skills listed and explained here are found in all of the activities in this resource.

Observing. Using all the senses to gather information about an object or happening. Your students will be better observers if they practice this skill often. Look at a frog. Feel it. Does the frog have a smell? Listen to its sounds. List its characteristics. Note changes from day to day. Does it have anything in common with a snake? A dog?

Classifying. Grouping objects according to basic similarities or common properties, looking for patterns. This process is the basis of much of our everyday life. Many classification systems are based on the observer's own ordering of things around him. Classifying is also the basis of biology and a primary tool for helping students to understand relationships.

Communicating. Relaying information from one person to another and reporting one's observations. Any observation, measurement, or prediction must be expressed to others in order that the ideas may be altered or expanded. Sharing information prepares students to work in every area of the curriculum.

Measuring. Using quantitative or dimensional qualities to assess certain properties of objects such as area, volume, height, and mass. This skill allows students to judge changes and gather information that can translate into mathematical terms.

Predicting. Using information already gathered to state in advance what will happen in the future: Students demonstrate the application of the early process skills with predicting. Now, careful observations, measurements, and discussions will allow them to be able to predict changes or outcomes of events.

Inferring. Forming a nonobservable judgment from an experience or observation. Inferring is not guessing. This judgment is based on information previously gathered and interpreted.

Hypothesizing. Forming a proposition as a basis for an argument or as a foundation for a conclusion. This is a more difficult skill as students team to make a statement and then attempt to prove the statement.

Experimenting. Testing done to confirm or deny a hypothesis or prediction, which involves methods of gathering data and additional information about the subject. In an experiment the student will learn to control variables and assess relationships between one object and another.

Collecting and analyzing data. Gathering of information based on observations, experiments, reading, field work, and constructing graphs, charts, maps, and tables that will help clarify the data and show relationships. The student will again be looking for patterns that develop and help explain a phenomenon.

Drawing conclusions. Summing up the outcome of a certain process, experiment, discussion, or observation that provides a deduction about the problem at hand. This process helps a student validate the reliability of the data.

Making generalizations. Inferring from the many particulars to reach a broad, sweeping universal application of the material at hand.

SECTION II
A Basic Introduction to Ecology

Background Information on Ecology

Ecology is a science that focuses on the study of organisms and their environment. The organization of these organisms may be studied on the levels of

1. populations—groups of individuals of one kind of organism
2. communities—groups of populations living in one place
3. the ecosystem itself—communities, the nonliving environment, and the flow of food and energy through the particular system

An individual organism along with others of its kind (a population) can be found in a particular location, the habitat, or place, where the established and surviving organisms live. This habitat and the organisms in it are influenced by factors such as light, temperature, water availability and type, density of the organisms, soil types and porosity, and availability of food. These factors are all abiotic, or nonliving, parts of the ecosystem. Food is available through a series of interactions, such as one organism eating another, forming a chain or food web. The community, all the populations in one place, is now of significance because it provides the basis for nutrition—the interaction between producers and consumers. The source of all of this movement of food, which is actually a flow of energy, is the Sun.

The concept of ecology, the study of the interactions between living organisms and their natural environment, is based upon three major principles:

1. Interaction occurs between producers (plants) and consumers (animals and decomposers), a universal feature of all ecosystems. This is sometimes called the ecology of nutrition.
2. There is a cyclic flow of matter through the planet's environment—water, carbon, nitrogen, and other elements are recycled and are used over and over again.
3. Energy keeps those matter cycles going, but it flows in a single direction. Energy enters the planet's atmosphere as sunlight and leaves the planet as heat.

Any changes, interruptions, or destructive action occurring within these patterns and relationships alter life on the planet Earth. Thus, what we do as humans, a population small in numbers compared to insects, for example—but one that consumes much of the food, energy, and matter on the planet—greatly affects what life will be like for all future inhabitants of Earth.

PART 1
Ecology

Concept Definition
Ecology is the science that studies the interactions and relationships that exist among living organisms with each other and their environment.

Objectives
The student will be able to
1. define ecology and discuss its applications to his or her own life
2. demonstrate a knowledge of basic ecological terms
3. explain the meaning of the biotic and abiotic factors within an environment and present examples of those influences in his or her own life
4. identify basic factors necessary for living

Process Skills
- Observing
- Describing
- Interviewing
- Generalizing
- Inferring
- Drawing conclusions
- Classifying
- Measuring
- Communicating

Topic: populations, communities, ecosystems
Go to: *www.scilinks.org*
Code: EXPL17

Topic: biotic and abiotic
Go to: *www.scilinks.org*
Code: EXPL18

National Science Education Content Standards addressed in this part:

Content Standard C
All organisms must be able to obtain and use resources, grow, reproduce, and maintain stable internal conditions while living in a constantly changing external environment.

An organism's behavior evolves through adaptation to its environment. How a species moves, obtains food, reproduces, and responds to danger are based on the species' evolutionary history.

A population consists of all individuals of a species that occur together in a given place and time. All populations living together and the physical factors with which they interact compose an ecosystem.

Content Standard E
Human populations include groups of individuals living in a particular location. One important characteristic of a human population is the population density—the number of individuals of a particular population that lives in a given amount of space.

ACTIVITY

At Issue

Introduction

As a means of introducing the immediate impact of the subject of ecology on students' lives, this first activity requires a search into ecological problems that need solutions. They may be either local problems or worldwide. At the conclusion of this activity, students should see a clear need for the study of ecology. You should lead them in a direction that entails a detailed study of many different parts of an affected area to find a solution. You can limit this activity to simple problems, or make it a comprehensive, in-depth exploration (see Activity 17).

From the NSES—p. 140

Changes in environments can be natural or influenced by humans. Some changes are good, some are bad, and some are neither good nor bad.

Objective

The student will be able to locate and define ecological problems and make reasonable suggestions that will lead to possible solutions.

Materials

- Student worksheet 1
- A collection of environmental articles from local and state newspapers, recent issues of national news magazines, or websites that you or your students have found. You can make collecting articles a homework assignment or you can begin directly by having the articles ready for any student to use—or just for those students who did not complete the assignment.

Teacher Instructions

1. Begin class discussion with the presentation of a classroom problem, such as not enough fresh air, overcrowding, loud noise level, unpopular seating arrangement, or the issues listed after the teacher instructions—any classroom environmental issue that can be discussed and has several possible solutions. Define this small problem as an integral part of their school environment.
2. Expand the discussion of environmental problems to the local community. Is there a place where kids throw their trash around school? Are there water use restrictions in town? Is a new building project under way that is taking away the habitat of animals?
3. Tell students to select an environmental problem or issue under discussion locally or at the state, national, or world level. Students should fill out student worksheet 1 as best they can, using newspapers, magazines, and on-site visits or interviews with people involved, if possible. Students should have a pertinent newspaper or magazine article to accompany their assessment of the problem.

4. Each student should present his or her issue, with class discussion after each presentation. Small groups with similar issues could be formed to discuss impact and solutions. In the discussion, a clear relationship needs to be made among the causes, impacts, and solutions of these problems. Roles in solutions can be discussed from two points of view, student and adult.

5. The newspaper and magazine articles should form the basis of a bulletin board display prepared by the class, entitled "Why Study Ecology?"

6. You may wish to expand this opening activity or return to it later in the unit, as a way to determine the changes that may have taken place in the way students think about their environment.

Other Issues Students Can Pursue

- Recycling
- Pollution
- Zoning
- Garbage and landfills
- Shortages
- Nuclear waste disposal
- Medical waste disposal
- Chemical waste disposal
- Soil erosion
- Effects of acid rain
- Endangered species
- Noise pollution
- Gasoline and fuel tank storage
- Air pollution
- Ocean dumping
- Rain forest destruction

At Issue

Locate a newspaper or magazine article about a national or local environmental problem or concern. Bring it to class. Discuss and/or answer the following:

1. Define the problem. _____
   _____

   _____

2. What are the causes of the problem? _____
   _____

   _____

   _____

   _____

3. Describe the environmental surroundings. _____
   _____

   _____

   _____

   _____

4. What is the impact of this problem on the area? _____
   _____

   _____

   _____

   _____

Interviewing to Determine the Definition of Ecology

Introduction

In this activity, students will find many different ideas of what ecology is, gathered from adults of their acquaintance, and compare the definitions they have gathered to the correct one.

Objective

The student will be able to determine the definition of ecology and explain the connections among various ideas about ecology.

Materials

- Student worksheet 2
- Chalkboard and chalk or large sheets of newsprint and wide felt-tip markers

Teacher Instructions

1. For homework the night before this activity, hand out student worksheet 2 and go over the directions with the students. Tell students to contact adults—relatives, neighbors, or other adults, but not peers—to explore various meanings of the word *ecology*. They may have the people they contact write their names and definition on the worksheet. Students may have to contact people by phone.

2. The next day, ask students to take out student worksheet 2, completed.

3. Ask students to give the name of one person interviewed and that person's definition of ecology. Record their answers on the chart. Try to list all definitions from students who volunteer.

4. Have students examine the master list. Ask them to pick out words or phrases that are repeated in more than one definition. Circle these.

5. Put these words and phrases into a correct definition of ecology, if possible. (Ecology is the science that studies the interaction and relationships that exist between organisms and their living and nonliving environment.)

6. If you wish, cut up all the student definitions and display them around the room. Students enjoy reading these and comparing them to the real definition they have learned.

Name _____ Date _____

Interviewing to Determine the Definition of Ecology

Ask five different adults (not other students in your classes) to define the word *ecology*. Write down the person's name and each definition given.

1. Name _____

   Definition _____

   _____

   _____

2. Name _____

   Definition _____

   _____

   _____

3. Name _____

   Definition _____

   _____

   _____

4. Name _____

   Definition _____

   _____

   _____

5. Name _____

   Definition _____

   _____

   _____

National Science Teachers Association

A Sensory Approach to Ecology

Introduction
This activity should make the students aware of the universality of ecological concerns. We include suggested readings or musical interpretations to use with this activity in the materials list, but you may want to use an artist of your own choice. There are many possibilities within the guidelines given.

From the NSES—p. 32
Recognize and respond to student diversity and encourage all students to participate fully in science learning.

Objective
The student will interpret the feelings and points of view of writers and artists who have an interest in the environment.

Materials
- Paper and pencil for each student
- Tape recorder, record player, or slide projector, if appropriate
- Audio suggestions
  - John Denver's "Rhymes and Reasons"
  - Aaron Copland's "Appalachian Spring"
- Reading suggestions
  - Rachel Carson's *Silent Spring*, part I, "A Fable for Tomorrow"
  - Ralph Waldo Emerson's "Woodnotes 1"
  - Dr. Seuss's *The Lorax*
- Visual suggestions
  - Any poster or painting reflecting the environment
  - Photographs by Ansel Adams
  - Sierra Club or Audubon Society posters
  - Old nature calendar prints
  - Slide show borrowed from museum or Audubon Society

Teacher Instructions
1. Discuss "points of view," how people feel about ecological issues and the different ways they act upon their feelings and convey their messages.
2. Suggest to the class that sometimes the messages aren't easy to understand and that each of us will interpret these messages in a slightly different way. There is no right or wrong answer.

ACTIVITY

3. Present the recordings, oral readings, slides, or pictures.

4. Have students listen to the presentation, taking notes if they wish. Encourage them not to compare notes.

5. Have students write their own interpretations of what they saw or heard in the presentations. A paragraph should suffice.

6. Collect all papers, and follow this with opinions and a general class discussion about the presentation. Tell students you will save their papers until the end of this unit of study, when you will return them so students can compare their understandings at the start of this unit with their understandings at the end of the unit.

7. When you have completed the ecology unit, repeat the entire activity by returning the students' papers to them, presenting the same artist, and then having students write their interpretations again. Compare. How have their attitudes and understanding changed?

Getting Started With Vocabulary

Introduction

Any new unit of study requires an introduction and the proper use of a concept vocabulary. Students should learn and use the correct terminology right from the beginning. Activities 4, 5, and 6 offer three different approaches to the ecology concept vocabulary. You may wish to use only one of them, saving the others to determine student retention later in the progress of the unit.

From the NSES—p. 144

The language evident in the classroom is an important element of doing inquiries.

Objective

The student will be able to explain and define basic ecology vocabulary.

Materials

- Student worksheet 4
- Pen or pencil for each student
- Books for finding definitions (text, trade, and/or dictionaries)

Teacher Instructions

1. Hand out student worksheet 4. Read the list of words so students will hear the correct pronunciation.
2. Have students locate definitions in resource material (or you may have students read "Planet Earth," the reproducible text section of Activity 6.) Students will understand the ecology vocabulary better if they write the definitions in their own words, rather than copying them from a glossary or dictionary.
3. Class discussions and constant use of these terms will make them part of the permanent vocabulary of your students.
4. Have students save this worksheet for future use. You may wish to correct their papers first.

Answers to Student Worksheet 4

- Environment—your surroundings
- Habitat—distinctive surroundings such as a pond
- Populations—a group of similar species in the same habitat, such as frogs or dandelions
- Food web—a network combining several food chains. One plant or animal may be eaten by a range of consumers
- Food chain—a series of events which link the food supply of plants and animals in a habitat

ACTIVITY

- Community—a group of organisms living in the same area
- Ecology—the study of the interactions of living and nonliving organisms in their environment
- Energy—potential forces in an ecosystem; the capacity for vigorous action
- Pollution—contamination
- Species—a plant or animal having distinct characteristics

Getting Started With Vocabulary

Define the following ecology terms using your own words.

1. Environment _____

_____

2. Habitat _____

_____

3. Populations _____

_____

4. Food web _____

_____

5. Food chain _____

_____

6. Community _____

_____

7. Ecology _____

_____

8. Energy _____

_____

9. Pollution _____

_____

10. Species _____

_____

 ACTIVITY

Ecology Vocabulary Crossword Puzzle

Introduction
An alternative method or further support for learning the ecology vocabulary is to use the crossword puzzle. Because students will not have a background in ecology yet, include the word list for them to use while completing the puzzle.

Objective
The student will be able to identify ecology vocabulary words and provide definitions of those words.

Materials
- Student worksheet 5 (crossword puzzle and word list)
- Pen or pencil
- Reference material (trade books, textbooks, dictionaries)

Teacher Instructions
1. Distribute the word list and the crossword puzzle to students.
2. Students should work on the crossword puzzle by matching word definitions to the words and fitting them into the puzzle.
3. When students complete the puzzle, discuss their answers and the word meanings. You may wish to use this word list later for a quiz.

Answers to the Crossword Puzzle
- Ecosystem—a community unit within its physical environment
- Omnivore—an organism that eats both plants and animals
- Energy pyramid—a pyramid structure to show how energy is used in a food chain
- Carbon cycle—oxygen and carbon going from plants to animals and back again in a continuous cycle
- Predator—an animal that feeds on other animals, usually kills prey
- Scavenger—an animal that feeds on dead animals, a consumer
- Biosphere—the broadest level of organization of living things
- Decomposer—microbe that causes decay or breakdown of dead plants and animals
- Herbivore—an organism that eats only plants
- Producer—an organism that makes its own food
- Water cycle—a continuous movement of water between Earth and air
- Carnivore—an organism that eats only animals
- Consumer—an animal that cannot make its own food and must eat plants and/or animals.

National Science Teachers Association

The crossword puzzle solution:

Across:
1. PRODUCER
4. SCAVENGER
6. CARBON CYCLE
8. HERBIVORE
9. OMNIVORE
10. PREDATOR
12. BIOSPHERE
13. WATER CYCLE

Down:
2. CONSUMER
3. DECOMPOSER
5. ENERGY PYRAMID
7. CARNIVORE
11. ECOSYSTEM

Name _____ Date _____

Ecology Vocabulary Crossword Puzzle Word List

Match the following words with the definitions given on your crossword puzzle sheets, write the definitions on the list below, and place the words in the correct position in the puzzle. Use dictionaries or textbooks if you need them.

1. Ecosystem _____

   _____

2. Omnivore _____

   _____

3. Energy pyramid _____

   _____

4. Carbon cycle _____

   _____

5. Predator _____

   _____

6. Scavenger _____

   _____

7. Biosphere _____

   _____

8. Decomposer _____

   _____

9. Herbivore _____

   _____

10. Producer _____

   _____

Name _____ Date _____ ⑤

11. Water cycle _____

_____

12. Carnivore _____

_____

13. Consumer _____

_____

Name _____ Date _____

Ecology Vocabulary Crossword Puzzle *

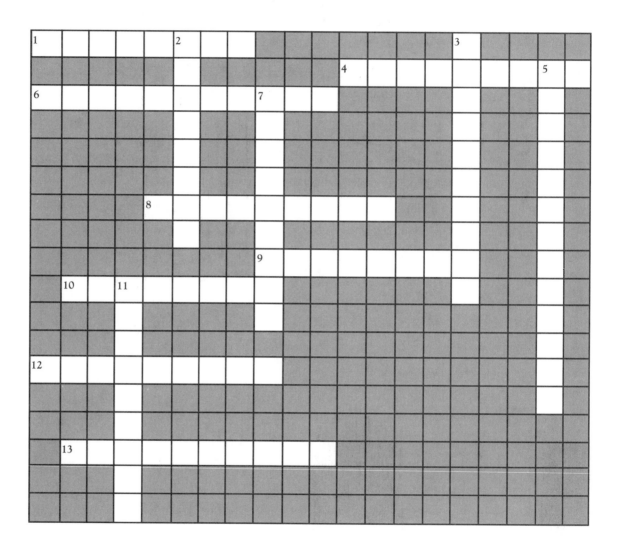

National Science Teachers Association

ACROSS

1. An organism that makes its own food
4. An animal that feeds on dead animals, a consumer
6. Oxygen and carbon going from plants to animals and back to plants in a continuous cycle (two words)
8. An organism that eats only plants
9. An organism that eats both plants and animals
10. An animal that feeds on other animals, usually kills prey
12. The broadest level of organization of living things
13. A continuous movement of water between Earth and air (two words)

DOWN

2. An animal that cannot make its own food and must eat plants and/or animals
3. Microbe that causes decay or breakdown of dead plants and animals
5. A pyramid structure to show how energy is used in a food chain (two words)
7. An organism that eats only animals
11. A community unit within its physical environment

*Permission granted by Mindscape, Inc.

Concept Mapping With Ecology Vocabulary

Introduction

Concept mapping is a study skill used to enhance meaningful learning. Not only does it provide a way for students to seek the pertinent information in written material or a lecture, but it also provides a means for the student to recreate the material in a diagrammatic, visual, concrete form.

Concept mapping is based on the theory of David Ausubel, an educational psychologist, that concepts derive meaning from connections or relationships with other concepts and that meaningful learning occurs when students link old information to new. Basically, there are three steps to concept mapping:

1. The student locates the main idea of an article, which may be a word or a sentence, and writes this word in the middle of a piece of paper. (In our activity, students could underline the main idea and supporting details first, since they are using worksheets and not textbooks.)
2. The student lists supporting details that clarify or extend the main idea. These details are then transferred to lines surrounding the main idea.
3. The student labels all lines with linking words that show how one detail relates to the main idea or to other details.

A sample concept map for student worksheet 6 is included, but it is important to remember that no two maps will be, nor should be, the same.

Objective

The student will define ecological terms and be able to explain the relationship among them.

Materials

- Student worksheet 6
- Pen or pencil
- "Planet Earth" handout

Teacher Instructions

1. Introduce the idea of concept maps to your students. If you have been using this study technique in other classes, this will be an extension of those activities. If not, perhaps this is a good exercise with which to begin teaching a new study skill.
2. Hand out student worksheet 6.
3. Follow the instructions on the student worksheet, steps 1 through 5. Caution students not to underline too much. The main idea of the text, "Planet Earth," is to explain some of the ideas and concepts behind the scientific study of the environment, i.e., ecology, the study of the relationship between organisms and their environment.

4. Because concept mapping is probably new to students, don't be too critical of their work. It is important for them to locate words like *environment, habitat, population, organisms, community, ecosystem, energy, consumer, producer, food chain, decomposer,* and *scavenger* and to begin to see that all these words relate to the study of ecology.

5. After all the maps are completed, you might want to ask several students put their work on the chalkboard or you might choose to display them around the room. Encourage comparison and emphasize that there are no "right" maps.

6. A sample concept map is on the next page.

Concept Map for Activity 6:

Concept Mapping With Ecology Vocabulary

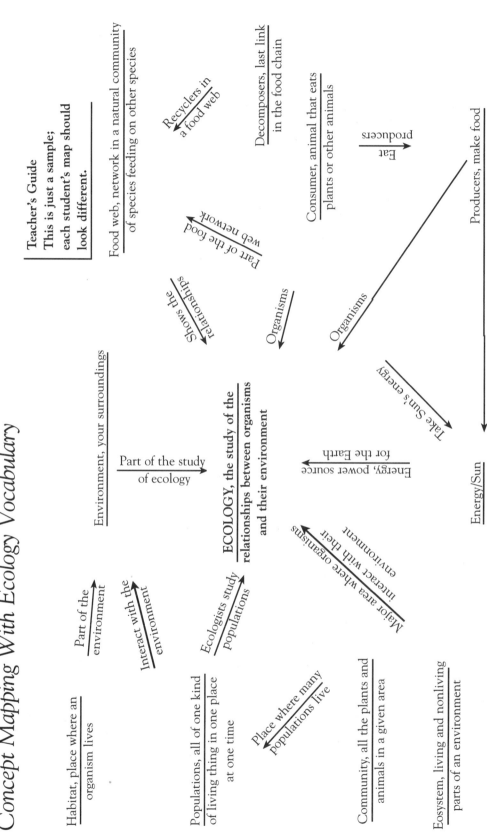

Teacher's Guide
This is just a sample;
each student's map should
look different.

Food web, network in a natural community of species feeding on other species

Recyclers in a food web

Decomposers, last link in the food chain

Consumer, animal that eats plants or other animals

Eat producers

Producers, make food

Part of the food web network

Shows the relationships

Organisms

Organisms

Take Sun's energy

Environment, your surroundings

Part of the study of ecology

ECOLOGY, the study of the relationships between organisms and their environment

Energy, power source for the Earth

Energy/Sun

Part of the environment

Interact with the environment

Ecologists study Populations

Major area where organisms interact with their environment

Habitat, place where an organism lives

Populations, all of one kind of living thing in one place at one time

Place where many populations live

Community, all the plants and animals in a given area

Ecosystem, living and nonliving parts of an environment

Concept Mapping With Ecology Vocabulary:

Instructions

Concept mapping is a study skill that will help you evaluate material you are reading for the first time. It is a tool to make learning more meaningful for you, and you can use it with any subject material. You will make a diagram of words (and pictures, if you wish) to help you remember this material. Follow the instructions carefully.

1. First, read through all of the material on ecology, "Planet Earth," without stopping.
2. Go back over the paragraphs and underline the main idea in each paragraph. Be careful not to underline too much. The main idea might be a whole sentence or only one word.
3. After you have finished underlining, look at the ecology map outline for this activity. Start with the main idea of "Planet Earth." In this activity, the main idea is already written into the diagram for you. Draw a circle around it.
4. Return to the text of "Planet Earth." Now you will be looking for supporting details, information that helps to explain the main idea. Underline any words or phrases that provide supporting information. For instance, the word *habitat* is part of the study of ecology. Habitat is a place where organisms live. You could write "habitat, a place where organisms live" on one of the lines around the main idea. Write these words on the lines on your paper. Draw connecting lines.
5. Now comes the hardest part. Take a minute and think of linking words, words that connect the supporting details and information to the main idea. Write these words on the connecting lines. These words should indicate the relationship between the main idea and supporting details. For example, a habitat is part of the environment, so you could draw a line between those two concepts and write that on it.
6. When you finish your map, you should have a good idea of the meaning of ecology and the vocabulary words that will become familiar to you as you study your surroundings.

 Name
 _____ Date _____

Concept Map

_____   _____

              _____

_____   ECOLOGY, the study of the
                               relationships between organisms
                               and their environment

                                                  _____

_____

_____   _____

              _____

National Science Teachers Association

Name _____ Date _____

Concept Mapping Text:
Planet Earth

You are alive today because this planet you live on provides the right conditions for your existence. Food comes from plants or the animals who eat those plants. Shelter and clothing come from natural elements and synthetic materials. The proper blend of gases for you to breathe is contained in the Earth's atmosphere. Water, the sustainer of life, is abundant on most parts of this planet. The Sun as the center of our solar system provides the energy to power the planet.

Yet all of these necessary parts of the Earth are limited in their supply. That means there is only a certain amount of water. We use and reuse the same water. We breathe and rebreathe the same oxygen atoms. Plants use and reuse the same nitrogen atoms.

Because our resources are limited, we need to take care of the place in which we live. To do that properly, we need to know everything we can about our planet Earth.

Ecology, a specialized field of science, is the study of the Earth's organisms and their relationship with each other, and the things around them that make up their environment. Ecology could be considered the most important science. Without a clear understanding of the interactions on Earth and the ways to protect those interactions, other progress will not matter. Let's take a closer look at Earth.

Earth is one huge environment made up of many smaller ones. Within each one of these places are many living and nonliving things. The living creatures interact with each other in a wide variety of ways. A polar bear has to eat something, so he has interactions with seals—hunting and killing them for a meal. Seals mate and raise their young, another kind of interaction. Another interaction occurs when bull elk fight for territory. Eating, reproducing, and fighting are just three of the many activities that living organisms engage in.

The nonliving parts of the environment are important, too. Could you, or the polar bear, live without water?

Within each environment there are particular habitats, or places where each organism lives. Some organisms live in the soil, some live in the water, some live on land, some live in the air. Where a particular creature lives is its habitat. A habitat can be seen and marked off. It may be as big as a sea or as small as the bottom of a rotten log.

Many organisms will live within one environment. These organisms will be divided into groups called populations. Populations are all the living things of the same kind (species) in one place at one time. A population may be as small as one polar bear living within a 100-mile area or 10 seals living in that same area or millions of plankton floating in the sea, also in that same area. Populations will vary in size from time to time, too. Some of the population may move away, or a population may have a birth explosion and greatly increase its numbers. Populations are studied as a whole, not as individuals.

A community is composed of groups of these different populations, both plants and animals, living together in one defined area and getting their food from somewhere in their environment. Communities may be as small as the aquarium in your classroom or as large as a pond or a lake.

The living creatures in a community must interact with each other. They must also interact with the nonliving parts of their environment. Together, the living community and the physical nonliving parts of the environment make up an ecosystem. All ecosystems have as their basis the Sun. The Sun provides the energy to power the system and make it work.

As the Sun shines on plants, the Sun's energy is converted into food. The plants are called producers. An animal cannot produce its own food. It must eat plants or other animals who have eaten plants to provide fuel for its body. The animal that relies on plants for its food is a consumer.

This flow of the Sun's energy forms a food chain:

SUN ENERGY ⟶ PLANT ENERGY ⟶ FOOD FOR ANIMALS
(ANIMAL ENERGY)

A drawing made of several food chains connected to each other would form a food web. A food web is a complicated diagram of many different kinds of animals eating many other animals or plants. A food web is a form of recycling. It is a way for food and energy to pass from one living thing to another, over and over again. How does that happen?

When one of the plants or animals dies, bacteria and fungi called decomposers, the last link in the food chain, begin to work. These organisms break down the dead remains and return the body components to the nonliving environment to be used again. The cycle starts all over.

Now that you have an understanding of how the planet Earth relies on balancing the interactions within its environment, you will be better able to continue your study of ecology. More and more our future existence will depend on keeping all of the parts of our environments protected so that living things will continue to exist.

Evaluating Basic Survival Requirements

Introduction

Students today seldom consider the essential things needed for survival as opposed to the items they have available for comfort. With careful encouragement, this activity will focus students on the difference between life as they know it and basic survival.

From the NSES—p. 129

An organism's patterns of behavior are related to the organism's environment.

Objective

The student will be able to determine the living and nonliving parts of an environment and discuss how life on Earth depends on each for survival.

Materials

- Student worksheet 7
- Pencil or pen

Teacher Instructions

1. Hand out student worksheet 7. Read the description of the setting so all students have the picture clearly in mind.
2. Have students complete numbers 1, 2, and 3 individually.
3. Form groups of five or six students. Each group should share individual answers for numbers 1, 2, and 3 and develop a group list.
4. Discuss group lists with the class by first listing items and then having the individual groups defend their selected and rejected items.
5. Numbers 4 and 5 are optional and should be used as time allows.
6. Return to the concept of the interdependence of living things in an environment and discuss from the point of view of survival in a community.
7. Relate survival to the community the students live in.
   - Where do the items necessary for survival come from? (Discuss air, water, food, shelter, and clothing.)
   - What happens if you run out? (Food shortages—people die, move, or adapt by learning to eat something else. For example, a bad frost in Florida forces Americans to drink something other than orange juice for breakfast or pay more for what is available. In the case of water contamination, we may buy water, purify water, or truck in water from outside the community. Be sure to discuss alternatives other than that the community dies or moves.)

- What can be done to preserve those items needed for survival? (Raising environmental awareness on the part of citizens, using the Environmental Protection Agency and governmental regulations, exercising individual responsibility, and taking individual action.)

7

What Do You Need to Survive?

The Situation

You are trekking in the mountains in early autumn. Unwisely, you have varied your course from the original plan. Therefore, no one knows where you are. An avalanche cuts off the trail behind you. There are more rumblings from above. Think fast!

1. Before the second rock slide hits, you have only moments to grab six items from your packhorse before you lose everything. Quickly choose from these:

food	jacket	rope	suntan lotion	rain gear
hatchet	plastic tarp	medicines	water in a jug	wool hat/mittens
hunting knife	jeans and T-shirt	snake-bite kit	blanket	toilet paper
bathing suit	knife, fork, spoon	sleeping bag	comic books	shotgun

2. Safe above the rockslide, your first job is to make a shelter to protect yourself from an approaching storm. List items you might find on the side of a mountain below the tree line that will allow you to survive until you are rescued.

Food: _____

_____

Recreation: _____

_____

Shelter: _____

_____

Clothing: _____

_____

Name _____ Date _____

3. Draw a picture of how you will arrange your campsite. Label everything.

4. Describe how you will arrange a signal if you spot rescue planes.

_____

_____

_____

_____

_____

_____

5. Perhaps you won't be found for weeks. Write a paragraph explaining how you plan to survive during that period. _____

_____

_____

_____

_____

_____

National Science Teachers Association

Examining the Living and Nonliving Parts of the Environment

Introduction

Students will quickly become aware of the parts of their environment in this simple, yet effective, experience. You will be introducing the terms *biotic* (living) and *abiotic* (nonliving) to the students in this activity.

From the NSES—pp. 157–158

See "Populations and Ecosystems."

Objective

The student will be able to identify living and nonliving parts of the environment and apply the new terms, *biotic* and *abiotic*, to them.

Materials

- Student worksheet 8
- Pen or pencil
- Large newsprint or chalkboard
- Markers or chalk

Teacher Instructions

1. Hand out student worksheet 8. Ask students to list immediately 15 items present in their inside environment. Items must be present to be listed although not necessarily seen (i.e., air). Encourage careful observation by discouraging listing of 15 students' names.

2. Now take students, without their talking or consulting with a friend, outside. Line them up in preparation for a 5- to 10-minute tour. During the tour, students should complete the bottom part of the worksheet listing 15 parts of the outside environment.

3. Discuss student findings when you return to the classroom. Make a master list for all to see of the items students listed inside and outside. Note careful and unusual observations.

4. Put the terms *biotic* and *abiotic* on the chalkboard. Discuss with students what it means to be a living or nonliving part of the surroundings. Ask students to look over their individual lists and mark all items with an "L" for living or an "N" for nonliving. Put these L's and N's on the master list. Discuss any disagreements.

5. Review the definition of ecology. Compare the number of L's to N's inside and outside. Discuss these numbers. (There should be many more living things outside than inside.) Elicit reasons from the students as to why the numbers are the way they are. What part do man-made versus natural environments play? Are students being accurate with the numbers? Have the students

ACTIVITY

counted each thing, or have they counted entire populations? (For instance, grass is really thousands of individual living things.)

6. If this activity is assigned as homework, be prepared to deal with a much wider variety of responses.

Examining the Living and Nonliving Parts of My Environment

List 15 things that you see or know are around you inside the classroom.

1. _____   9. _____
2. _____   10. _____
3. _____   11. _____
4. _____   12. _____
5. _____   13. _____
6. _____   14. _____
7. _____   15. _____
8. _____

List 15 things that you see or know are around you outdoors.

1. _____   9. _____
2. _____   10. _____
3. _____   11. _____
4. _____   12. _____
5. _____   13. _____
6. _____   14. _____
7. _____   15. _____
8. _____

ACTIVITY

Differentiating Living and Nonliving Parts of the Environment

Studying Drawings of Pond, Forest, and Meadow Environments

Introduction

In this activity, students will use drawings of up to three different environments to determine the living and nonliving parts of those environments. First, students will identify and list parts of the environment in each drawing. Although they should strive for accuracy and specific identification, it is more important that numbers of the living and nonliving parts of these environments are clear rather than the species' names. The interrelationships that will be made will rely more on the numbers than on the specific population names.

From the NSES—pp. 157–158

See "Populations and Ecosystems."

Objective

Students will apply information learned about the biotic and abiotic factors of an environment to new environments. Students will discuss the interrelationships of these factors.

Materials

- Student worksheets 9 and one or more of 9A, 9B, or 9C
- Pen or pencil
- Optional: transparencies of the pond, meadow, and forest drawings for use with an overhead projector.

Teacher Instructions

1. Review with your students the difference between living and nonliving parts of an environment (see Activity 8).
2. Hand out student worksheets 9 and one or more of 9A, 9B, or 9C.
3. Have students identify all items in the drawing or drawings and write the names of these items in the space provided at the bottom. Students should work on their lists until they have identified all objects, or as many as possible.

4. Have students, with as many participating as possible, name the parts of the environment. Refer to the teacher copy if species names are not familiar. Students may add to their lists those items they omitted or were not able to identify. When you are satisfied that lists are complete, continue.

5. Have each student go through the completed lists and label each item with an "L" for living or an "N" for nonliving.

6. When students complete the labeling, ask them to count the number of L's and N's and record this data at the bottom of the worksheet. Compare these numbers with Activity 8.

7. Then tell students to answer questions 5a through 5f on their worksheets. Discuss these questions when everyone has finished. (See answer section at the end of the teacher instructions.)

8. Student worksheets 9A (pond), 9B (forest), and 9C (meadow) all use the instructions on student worksheet 9. They can all be used in the same way or you can choose to use them as a homework assignment, quiz, or rainy-day activity. If you do have students complete more than one of these environments, you can discuss why one species lives in a certain environment and not in another.

Answers to Student Worksheet 9 Questions

5a. What is ecology? (The science that studies the interactions and relationships that exist between organisms and their living and nonliving environment.)

5b. What parts of an environment are called biotic? (The living things.)

5c. What parts of an environment are called abiotic? (The nonliving things.)

5d. What are other factors that could affect this environment? (People, pollution, overpopulation, weather changes, construction, etc.)

5e. What effect could any one or all of these factors have on this environment? (It is likely that any one or all of these factors would alter or change the environment in some way. For instance, human activity could eliminate most of the biotic parts by building roads, constructing houses, or other invasive actions. Serious drought or prolonged, cold winters could kill many of the plants that the animals require as food sources.)

5f. Should this environment be protected in any way? Why or why not? (Individual responses will vary based on the answers to 5e.)

Living and Nonliving Parts of the Pond

Animals
A. Eastern painted turtle
B. Water striders
C. Stoneflies
D. Sunfish
E. Northern pike
F. Great blue heron
G. Belted kingfisher
H. Beaver
I. Ruddy duck

Plants
1. Common cattails
2. Pickerel weed
3. Fragrant water lilies
4. Grey birch
5. Maple
6. Balsam fir

Possible nonliving items
Air (gases)
Soil
Rock
Water
Log
Dead twigs

L = ——————————————   N = ——————————————

50

Living and Nonliving Parts of the Forest

Animals
A. Eastern milk snake
B. Chestnut-sided warbler
C. Gray squirrel
D. Raccoon
E. White-tailed deer
F. Red-tailed hawk
G. Northern three-toed woodpecker
H. Red fox
I. Ant
J. Tick
K. Stag beetle

Plants
1. Balsam fir
2. Spruce
3. Beech
4. Red pine

Possible nonliving items
Soil
Air (gases)
Water
Rocks
Dead trees

L = ———————————   N = ———————————

51

Living and Nonliving Parts of the Meadow

Animals:
A. Eastern meadowlark
B. Sulphur butterfly
C. Praying mantis
D. Grasshopper
E. Ladybug
F. Inchworm
G. Eastern chipmunk
H. Eastern mole

Plants
1. Bindweed
2. Black-eyed Susans
3. Quack grass
4. Bent grass
5. Chicory
6. Goldenrod
7. Lupine

Possible nonliving items:
Water
Soil
Air (gases)
Dead or decaying plant material
Fence

L = ——————————   N = ——————————

9

Differentiating Living and Nonliving Parts of an Environment

Your task will be to identify the living and nonliving parts of the environments in the drawing you are given.

1. In the space below the drawing, list the names of all the things you see in the picture. For instance, in the pond environment picture, you might list turtle, great blue heron, cattails, and many more.

2. Look closely at the drawing: Include both the living and nonliving parts of the community on your list.

3. When you finish your list, your teacher will ask all students to share the names of things identified from the drawings. From this discussion, add the names of anything you do not already have on your own list.

4. Now label each item on your list with an "L" for living or an "N" for nonliving. Count the number of L's and N's. Put the total of each group at the bottom of the list.

5. Answer the following questions:

    a. What is ecology? _____

        _____

        _____

    b. What parts of an environment are called biotic? _____

        _____

        _____

    c. What parts of an environment are called abiotic? _____

        _____

        _____

    d. What are the other factors that could affect this environment? _____

        _____

        _____

Name _____ Date _____

e. What effect would any one of these factors have on this environment? Would that be good or bad? Why? _____

_____

_____

f. Should this environment be protected in any way? Why or why not?

_____

_____

Name _____ Date _____

Living and Nonliving Parts of the Pond

L = _____   N = _____

Name _____ Date _____

Living and Nonliving Parts of the Forest

L = _____   N = _____

Name _____ Date _____

Living and Nonliving Parts of the Meadow

L = _____   N = _____

PART 2
Populations

Concept Definition
A population is a group of the same kind of organisms in a given space at a given time.

Objectives
The student will be able to
1. define population
2. estimate populations in a community
3. count and compare populations within a community
4. describe plant and animal populations living in a community
5. experiment with plant populations to control growth and development
6. discuss the effects of abiotic conditions on a community

Process Skills
- Classifying
- Measuring
- Observing
- Inferring
- Hypothesizing
- Experimenting

Topic: **populations, communities, ecosystems**
Go to: *www.scilinks.org*
Code: **EXPL17**

National Science Education Content Standards addressed in this part:

Content Standard A
Identify questions that can be answered through scientific investigations.

Use mathematics in all aspects of scientific inquiry.

Content Standard C
A population consists of all individuals of a species that occur together at a given time and place.

The number of organisms an ecosystem can support depends on the resources available and the abiotic factors such as light and water, range of temperatures, and soil composition.

Populations of organisms can be categorized by the function they serve in an ecosystem. Plants and some microorganisms are producers—they make their own food. All animals, including humans, are consumers, which obtain food by eating other organisms. Decomposers, primarily bacteria and fungi, are consumers that use waste materials and dead organisms for food. Food webs identify the relationships among producers, consumers, and decomposers in an ecosystem.

ACTIVITY

Estimating and Counting Populations

Introduction

This is a teacher directed activity. If you plan to have your students participate in Activity 11, that activity will go more smoothly with this work done as preparation. If you are not able to use both activities, this work will give students a basic background for counting and estimating a population. The first part of this activity develops materials for a bulletin board display.

From the NSES

Plan and conduct a simple investigation, p. 122.
See "Populations and Ecosystems," pp. 157–158.

Objective

The student will identify specific populations and compare two methods for counting populations.

Materials

- Stack of old magazines (one per student)
- Drawing paper
- Markers or crayons
- Ruler
- Pencil
- Student worksheet 10

Teacher Instructions

1. Review definition of a population with your students. (A population is a group of the same kind of organisms in a given space at a given time. Remind students that organisms are living things, both plants and animals.)
2. Instruct students to search through magazines until they each locate a picture that illustrates the definition of a population. Students should cut out the picture, identify and count the population, and record this information on the drawing paper. (For example, one student may have 25 trees; another, 3 people.)
3. Students should then staple their population pictures and numbers information onto the bulletin board.
4. Briefly discuss and compare the completed bulletin board with the definition of a population. Do the students' examples fit the definition?
5. Discuss the problems a scientist might have in counting populations in nature. (Animals move, the space is too large for accurate counting, organisms are too small to count, too many organisms, only a very few organisms.)

6. Distribute student worksheet 10. The two methods of population counting that students will practice are the actual counting method and the grid method.

7. On student worksheet 10 there is an illustration of a small section of a pond community. Pictured are three different populations: pond lilies, cattails, and ducks. Students should identify populations and record the information on the chart below the illustration.

8. Students should then count each population and record the data in the appropriate space on their chart beside the words *actual count*.

9. Discuss the following questions:
   a. Which population was the easiest to count? (Ducks) Why? (Large organisms, only a few of them. In an actual pond, however, these animals might be flying.)
   b. Which population was the most difficult to count? (Cattails) Why? (Too many, varying sizes.)
   c. Can anyone think of a way to count cattails without counting each individual one? (Estimation)

10. The following directions introduce the grid method of estimating populations:
   a. Using the rulers, students should measure the length of the pond (about 6 inches) and the width of the pond (about 2 inches).
   b. Students should draw a rectangle encompassing the boundaries of the pond and then mark off a grid of 1-inch squares.
   c. To use the grid method for estimation, students count the population of cattails in any one segment of the grid. They then multiply that number by the number of squares in the entire grid. (Example: 10 cattails x 12 grid squares = 120 cattails.)

11. Students should use the grid method to estimate all three of the assigned populations and record the data on the chart under the grid. (It will be possible to get a population count of 12 or 0 for the ducks, for instance, by this method. This problem will be discussed in question 6c on the student worksheet.)

12. Discuss the answers to these questions from the student worksheet to close the activity:
   a. When did this grid method of counting populations work? (It was successful for cattails—a large, stationary population.) When did it not work? (It did not work for ducks. The results were either too large or too small.)
   b. Which population counting method (actual count or grid) do you consider to be more accurate? (Answers will vary. It depends on the situation, location, and species being counted.) Why?
   c. Why must ecologists use the grid method to count some populations? (It would take forever, and still be inaccurate, to count all the grass plants in the front lawn.)
   d. When would the grid method not work? (It would not work with animals that are alive and moving or when there are only a small number of a species present.)
   e. Describe a solution that scientists have devised to solve this last problem. (Banding or tagging, technically called the recapture method.)

Estimating and Counting Populations

This activity will teach you about counting a population. You will compare two methods, actual count method and grid method, that are used by ecologists to assess the populations in a community.

Population name			
Actual count			
Grid count			

1. The picture above is an illustration of a small section of a pond community. Identify the three most abundant populations you can see. Record the name of each population on the chart below the picture.

2. The first method for counting a population is called actual count. Count each population one by one. Record that data beneath the identified group on the chart beside the words *actual count*.

3. Answer these questions:
   a. Which population was the easiest to count? Why?

   _____

   _____

10

  b. Which population was the most difficult to count? Why?

  _____

  _____

  c. Suggest a way to count the most difficult population without counting each individual one.

  _____

  _____

4. The second method for counting a population is called the grid method. To make a grid, follow these steps:
   a. Place your ruler against the bottom edge of the pond picture. Draw a line long enough to include all of the pond edges.
   b. Put your ruler against the right edge of the pond picture. Draw a line up until you are above the top edge of the pond.
   c. Connect the top, bottom, and sides to complete a rectangle around your drawing.
   d. Divide your rectangle into sections 1-inch square. You now have a grid. Count the total squares in your grid. There are _____ squares in my grid.

5. To use your grid for counting populations, you will count the population in only one square.
   a. Choose one square at random. For this first example, count the water lilies in that square.
      There are _____ water lilies in my square.
      There is a total of _____ squares in my grid.
   b. To estimate the water lily population in the entire pond, multiply the number of water lilies in one square times the total squares in the grid. Record this data on the chart beside the words *grid count*.
   c. Repeat this process for cattails and ducks and record the data.

6. Answer these questions from your grid method work.
   a. When did this grid method of counting populations work? When did it not work?

   _____

   _____

Name _____ Date _____

b. Which population counting method (actual count or grid) do you consider more accurate? Why?

_____

_____

c. Why do ecologists use the grid method to count some populations?

_____

_____

d. When would the grid method not work?

_____

_____

e. What is another method that scientists use for counting moving populations when the grid method won't work?

_____

_____

_____

National Science Teachers Association

A Field Study:
Counting Populations

Introduction

A population is all of the living things of one kind in the same habitat. Begin this lesson by reviewing the definition of a population and have the students give as many examples of populations as you think necessary to be sure the students understand the idea of population. If possible, have each student give an example.

From the NSES—p. 157–158

See "Populations and Ecosystems."

Objective

The student will be able to define population, give examples of populations, and discuss why populations are difficult to count.

Materials

- Student worksheet 11
- Populations of the school by grade level
- Your list of local plant and animal populations
- Large newsprint and markers

Teacher Instructions

IMPORTANT: Read "Health and Safety in the Field," p. 12, before you carry out this activity with students.

1. You will need to compile a list of populations native to the local community in order to complete this activity. Choose plants and animals which live around the school area and list them on the student worksheet before it is duplicated. (A list of sample populations follows.) Equal numbers of plants and animals are helpful. This activity uses the school population by grade level. Usually the school secretary will have this information.

    Suggested items for population lists: grass, dandelions, maple, oak, pine, beech, other trees, robins, crows, flies, mosquitoes, frogs, skunk cabbage, horsetails, water striders if your school is near a pond, bluets, butterflies, pedestrians, squirrels, ferns, plantain, gnats, slugs, and clover. Remember, populations may be any size, but must be of living things.

2. Pupils begin by counting the students in their group and recording that information on the worksheet. Provide them with the population information for their school. Students should then complete the definition of a population.

3. Place students in teams of two, and assign each team a population to count outside the school building. This teaming will go smoothly if you have a master sheet listing the population next to the names of each team. It is especially important to match the ability of a student team to a reasonable type of a population. Students in accelerated math classes will be more able to deal with counting grass, while students who may have difficulty with these skills should be assigned a simple item to count. (See Table 11.) Avoid having more than one team count the same population. Make sure all students know what their populations look like.

4. Discuss the rules for counting.
   a. Set boundaries of the area so that all students are counting in the same place.
   b. Briefly discuss what to do if students are counting a large population such as grass. (See Activity 10.) This is an opportunity to teach math.
   c. Set a time limit and a signal that will end the outside activity. (A whistle is good.) Allow at least 10 minutes to return to class.

5. Upon returning to class students should complete the questions on the worksheet page while the teacher sets up the master chart, which will include all teams, populations, and numbers. Record all numbers on the master chart exactly as reported.

Table 11 Sample Master Chart

Plant			Animals		
Team	Population	#	Team	Population	#
Fran/Tom	grass	4,682,102	Mary/Kay	frogs	6
Sue/Jen	maple trees	28	Jim/Bill	mosquitoes	87
Jake/Pat	dandelions	523	Heidi/Molly	robins	0

6. Discuss the numbers of populations and the reasons why the variety occurs. (Sizes of plants and animals, i.e., flies versus cows or trees versus grass; abiotic factors in the community like temperature, soil, wind, and water.)

7. Discuss questions 6 to 9 on the student worksheet (see answer section that follows).

Answers to Student Worksheet 11

6. How do the following populations affect each other?
   > A. robins and B. earthworms
   > A. caterpillars and B. trees
   > A. frogs and B. flies

   (One eats the other; the prey decreases in numbers; some predators have to move to find more food.)

7. What would happen if the A population became very large? (It would deplete the B population and starve or move.)

8. What would happen if the B population became very large? (More predators could exist in the area; B population could become pests; whatever populations B population eats would decrease; some B population would die, move, or adapt.)
9. When do you think each pair of populations in list A and B is in balance? Explain your answer. (This is a question for speculation; listen to all answers.)

Name _____ Date _____

A Field Study:

Counting Populations

1. Count the number of pupils in your class.

Girls _____

Boys _____

Total _____

2. What is the population of your school?

Grade _____

Grade _____

Grade _____

Grade _____

Total _____

Name _____ Date_____

3. What is a population? _____

    _____

    _____

Your Assignment:
As a class you will be divided into teams of two pupils each. Each team will be assigned to count a certain population found in the area around the school within a certain time. You must count only in that area and only within the time limit.

Record your results on the chart below.

Your names	Plant or animal populations	Total number

When you have finished counting, answer these questions.

4. Was your population easy or hard to count? Why? _____

    _____

    _____

    _____

5. Did you count or estimate your population?

    _____

    _____

Name _____ Date _____

6. How do the following populations under A and B affect each other?

A		B
robins	and	earthworms
caterpillars	and	trees
flies	and	frogs

_____

_____

_____

_____

7. What would happen if the A populations became very large?

_____

_____

8. What would happen if the B populations became very large?

_____

_____

9. When do you think each pair of populations in Lists A and B is in balance? Explain your answer.

_____

_____

_____

_____

_____

Experimenting With Overpopulation I

Introduction
This experiment graphically demonstrates what happens to a community under the pressures of a population increase.

From the NSES
Display and demand respect for the diverse ideas, skills, and experiences of all students, p. 136. See "Populations and Ecosystems," pp. 157–158.

Objective
The student will experience the pressures of overpopulation and will be able to explain animal behavior as a result of overpopulation.

Materials
- Paper and pencil for each student
- A topic for a writing assignment. (Examples: what I plan to do in the future, what life will be like 50 years from now, why the science of ecology is important to this planet.)

Teacher Instructions
1. Give the writing assignment. Place a stipulation on the assignment, such as saying that a significant part of the grade for the quarter depends on how well and thoughtfully the student writes this short essay. Let students write for about 30 seconds.
2. Interrupt students, and ask a few to move their chairs and join another group at a table (or limit the space for desks) forcing them to form a larger population in a smaller space. Students must bring their writing assignments with them, and they must have it in contact with a desk or table when they have moved. The teacher must remain serious throughout this change and not allow conversation.
3. Continue to create a situation where students are cramped and crowded, but in which they feel they must do a good job at their assignment.
4. After 3 to 5 minutes have the students stop writing, and, before they return to their seats, discuss how they feel right at that moment. Ask questions that cause students to look at their behavior—fighting, squirming, feeling angry or upset, trying to get away.
5. Have students return to their regular seats. Discuss what happens when one population becomes too large for the habitat it lives in.
6. Discuss what choices individuals have in an overpopulated situation. (Die, adapt, or move. How?) This discussion can be related to overpopulation in a community as in Activity 14.

Note: Be sensitive to the emotional threshold of your students. Unless students really know and trust you, some of the more conscientious students could become frustrated and overwrought by having their attempts thwarted after they have been told how important this activity will be in determining grades. This worked well for us when we worked with the students in April and May one year. Another teacher had a difficult time when she taught the unit in September.

Experimenting With Overpopulation II

Introduction

Students sometimes think only humans and animals constitute populations and forget plants. In this experiment, you will use a planting activity to reinforce the concept of population and the biotic and abiotic factors that are basic for growth and development in various populations. This experiment can be done in a number of different ways:

- You can skip all the planting procedures and purchase two flats of plants (petunias, calendula, broccoli) and proceed from there.
- The planting and record keeping can be done by a small group of students and the results shared with the class.
- You can divide the students into small teams of three or four each, and each group can proceed with the entire experiment comparing results.
- With older students, this experiment can be developed into a project that examines growth factors—amount of light, amount of water, fertilizer, acid water (rain) effects, crowding conditions, seed varieties; ability to withstand adverse conditions, or putting two types of seeds in one pot (so that students observe the effects of one population on another).

From the NSES

Create a setting for student work that is flexible and supportive of science inquiry, p. 43.
See "Populations and Ecosystems," pp. 157–158.

Objective

The student will be able to observe and describe conditions required for maximum growth of certain plant populations. The student will be able to suggest ways to improve the plant population's growth and well-being.

Materials

- 2 equal-size containers for plants for each student (pots or flat trays)
- Soil
- Seeds (any type that germinates quickly, e.g., curly cress, calendula, tomato, marigold)
- Masking tape for marking each container
- A sunny window
- Standard measure for water
- Student worksheet 13

ACTIVITY

Teacher Instructions

1. Provide each student or team with two plant containers, adequate soil, and seeds. Mark each container with an "O" for overpopulated or "B" for balanced. Students should follow the instructions on student worksheet 13.

2. Pots should be checked daily. Water both pots with equal amounts of water, using a standard measure.

3. After germination, the students should leave the O container alone, but should thin the plants in the B container after the plants have developed root systems to make ample room between each plant. This needs to be done carefully. Germination time varies; students can refer to information on seed packets for more definitive data.

4. Students should keep the plants in a sunny location and water as necessary, always in equal amounts to simulate equal rainfall.

5. Once a week students should measure the tallest (or several tallest) plants in each container, and record the results and any comments they might have on the chart in student worksheet 13.

6. After a few weeks, depending on the growth rate of the plants, the teacher should direct the students to answer section 5 on their worksheets. At this point, class time should be devoted to demonstrations of the experiments and class discussion as to the best conditions for a population's survival and a population's growth and development.

National Science Teachers Association

Name _____ Date _____

Experimenting With Overpopulation

This is an experiment in which you will prepare a population of plants, observe their growth, and then list the factors that you think are necessary for growth and development of your plant population.

1. Plant seeds close together (about 6 per square inch) in two equal-size containers. Mark one container "O" for overpopulated and one "B" for balanced. Check soil, and provide equal amounts of water regularly before germination.

2. After plants germinate, pull out most of the plants in the B containers so that each plant left has plenty of space around it. Do not touch the plants in the O container.

3. Continue to water regularly with equal amounts of water. Keep both containers in sunlight.

4. Check plants each week. Measure the size of the tallest plant or plants in each container. Record your comments as to the condition of plants in each container on Chart 13A.

5. After a few weeks, answer the following questions about your experiment: How was the growth of the plants in B and O similar? _____

    _____

    _____

    How was their growth different? _____

    _____

    _____

    Which plants appear the healthiest? Why? _____

    _____

    _____

    Did any plants die? If so, why do you think that happened? _____

    _____

    _____

Name _____ Date _____

What do you think are the best conditions for plant growth? _____

_____

_____

What biotic and abiotic factors did both sets of plants require? _____

_____

_____

Name _____ Date_____

Results of Plant Overpopulation Experiment

	BALANCED			OVERPOPULATED		
Week #	Size	General appearance	Comments	Size	General appearance	Comments

Role Playing:
Populations and the Balance of Nature

Introduction

This activity will illustrate for your students some of the relationships of plants, animals, and people in an environment, with special emphasis on the balance of nature.

The students will assume the roles of rabbits, hawk, hunter, and foxes. You must act as a facilitator by identifying students and roles, calling for action, and leading the discussion to make clear the relationships occurring and changing as the scene unfolds.

From the NSES

Engage students in designing the learning environment, p. 43.
See "Populations and Ecosystems," pp. 157–158.

Objective

The student will be able to discern and discuss the factors that may cause overpopulation in a community.

Materials

None

Teacher Instructions

1. Ask students to describe everything they know about wild rabbits—color, size, shape, food, how they move, enemies. If they offer information on pet rabbits, make sure they are aware of the differences in the wild. For instance, rabbits eat carrots, but generally carrots are not found in a natural habitat. What would they eat instead? Have six students stand up. They will assume the roles of rabbits in this environment. They are *herbivores*.
2. Choose one student to play the role of a hawk. Identify the characteristics of hawks. Of particular importance in this activity is the fact that hawks will eat small mammals such as rabbits. Hawks are *carnivores*.
3. Another student will assume the role of the hunter. Discuss the reasons for hunting. For instance, it helps control populations and provides food and sport for people. At this point, the hunter "shoots" the hawk and the person playing the hawk sits down.
4. The hunter goes home (sits down). Discuss briefly that it is against the law to shoot birds of prey.
5. Emphasize the environment as it now exists. Discuss the breeding habits of rabbits. Ask rabbits to pair up to become a rabbit family.

6. Each rabbit pair should now select four baby rabbits from the class.

7. At the end of this "family-generating session," stop the activity and discuss what will begin to happen to the plants that rabbits eat now that there has been a change in the hawk population of this community.

8. Have the baby rabbits each choose a partner rabbit. Discuss the same issue as in number 7 while considering the increase in the rabbit population. Make sure to include these questions:

   a. If nothing changes, what do you predict will happen to the number of plants in the community? Why?

   b. If nothing changes, what do you predict will happen to the number of rabbits in the community? Why?

   c. What other carnivores might exist in this community? Would they feed on rabbits?

   d. What will have to happen to have the balance of nature restored to this community?

9. Choose a fox family composed of a fox, a vixen, and two kits. Discuss fox food and habits. (All rabbits hold their positions.)

10. Have each fox call the name of a rabbit that he or she has eaten. Those students sit down. Ask the students: How long will it take for the community to right itself if the foxes continue to live there?

11. Continue the role-play for as long as you wish. This activity creates the opportunity for student research on the effect of population changes on a community. For example, a rabbit population explosion was felt in a part of Australia, an island continent. Rabbits were imported to balance an undesirable weed population. Because there were few natural predators, the rabbit population flourished. Australia is noted for sheep and cattle stations. Of course, the economy of those industries was in danger due to grassland depletion by the rabbits. A bounty was offered, the rabbit population reduced, and the balance of nature returned.

12. Have students then apply these ideas to a familiar setting: Suppose 300 new families moved into your town. All of the children would come to your school. What problems would surface at school? (Overcrowded classes, not enough books or desks, reduced space in the lunchroom.) What problems would occur in the community? (Not enough houses, more traffic, more trash generated.) Are there any good things that result from a human population increase? (An increase in tax revenues for the town, new faces, and new ideas for the community.)

PART 3
Communities

Concept Definition

A community is composed of groups of different populations (plants and animals) living together in one defined area or habitat and obtaining food energy from somewhere in their surroundings.

SCiLINKS.
THE WORLD'S A CLICK AWAY

Topic: populations,
communities,
ecosystems
Go to: *www.scilinks.org*
Code: EXPL17

Objectives

The student will be able to do the following:

1. define a community
2. examine a map, identify boundaries of a community, and predict what populations may or may not be present
3. make inferences about what factors make a community a success
4. debate the pros and cons of ecological decisions of a community
5. survey small communities around their own school building
6. experiment with conditions required for community survival and predict outcomes
7. examine a soil sample, name and classify the soil type, determine soil porosity, and measure and graph temperatures

Process Skills

- Measuring
- Classifying
- Experimenting
- Communicating
- Drawing conclusions
- Collecting and analyzing data
- Making generalizations
- Observing
- Inferring
- Predicting
- Hypothesizing

National Science Education Content Standards addressed in this part:

Content Standard A

- Identify questions that can be answered through scientific investigations.
- Design and conduct a scientific investigation.
- Use appropriate tools and techniques to gather analyze and interpret data.
- Develop descriptions, explanations, and models using evidence.
- Think critically and logically to make the relationships between evidence and explanations.
- Recognize and analyze alternative explanations and predictions.
- Use mathematics in all aspects of scientific inquiry.

Content Standard C

The world has many different environments and distinct enviroments support the life of different types of organisms.

A population consists of all individuals of a species that occur together at a given place and time. All populations living together and the physical factors with which they interact compose an ecosystem.

The number of organisms an ecosystem can support depends on the resources available and abiotic factors such as quantity of light and water, range of temperatures, and soil composition. Given adequate biotic and abiotic resources and no disease or predators, populations (including humans) increase at rapid rates. Lack of resources and other factors such as predation and climate limit the growth of populations in specific niches in the ecosystem.

Content Standard D

Soil consists of weathered rocks and decomposed organic material from dead plants, animals, and bacteria. Soils are often found in layers with each having a different chemical composition and texture.

Content Standard F

When an area becomes overpopulated the environment will become degraded due to the increased use of resources.

Internal and external earth processes of the earth system cause natural hazards, events that change or destroy wildlife habitats, damage property, and harm or kill humans.

Human activities also can induce hazards through resource acquisition, urban growth, land use decisions, and waste disposal. Such activities can accelerate many natural changes.

Exploring Your Community With a Map

Introduction
This activity will make your students look at the community in which they live by using a map of their town or city. They will be asked to determine the boundaries, natural or artificial, and to identify some of the plant and animal populations that live in the community.

From the NSES—p. 44
Make the available science tools, materials, media, and technological resources accessible to students.

Objective
The student will examine a map of his or her community, identify boundaries, and predict some of the populations that may or may not live there.

Materials
- Completed vocabulary student worksheet 4 (optional)
- Student worksheet 15
- A map of your community for each group of students (outdated maps are often available free from the Chamber of Commerce or your local library)
- Pen or pencil

Teacher Instructions
1. Begin this lesson with an introduction or a review of these vocabulary words:
   a. *Community*—groups of different populations (plant and animal) living together in one defined area or habitat.
   b. *Populations*—organisms of the same kind living in the same community.
   c. *Boundary*—anything natural or manmade that marks a limit.
   At the end of the vocabulary discussion, tell the group they are going to explore the community they live in using a map.
2. Hand out student worksheet 15 and the community maps. Students may work in groups of two or three for this activity. Each student, however, should complete his or her own worksheet.
3. Have students read the directions to Part 1. You may want to help them with the first activity of locating boundaries. Natural boundaries are easy to locate (rivers, lakes, mountain ranges), but artificial boundaries are difficult for students to decide upon, especially if the lines are arbitrarily drawn. Try to locate major roads or thoroughfares for boundaries. Exact boundaries are not as important in this activity as the idea of seeing the whole community, which will then be separated into smaller sections.
4. As students finish Part I, you may wish to stop and discuss what they have learned about the community. It is especially fun to discuss what will live and what cannot live in the community naturally and the reasons why. (For instance, prickly pear cactus does not grow in a large portion of the United States. Climate, moisture, and soil conditions are determining factors.)

5. When you begin Part II you will use your school as one of the smaller communities within the large town or city. The information that students provide here can be used as the basis for continuing community activities in this section when you work outside with the students (Activities 18 and 21).

6. Students should answer all questions in Part III at the end of their worksheets. The followup discussion will emphasize the reasons why plants and animals live where they do. (The environment must provide the necessary things for organisms to carry on their life activities of eating, finding shelter, reproducing, and providing protection.)

7. You may wish to extend the discussion to include what will happen if the habitat becomes polluted. The populations will
    a. adapt (discuss how)
    b. die (discuss why)
    c. move to another place

    Do students know of a part of your community where pollution has occurred with these results? (See Activity 1, "At Issue.")

15

Exploring Your Community With a Map

Part I:

1. Spread your map out on a flat surface.

2. Locate the boundaries of your community. Boundaries separate your city (community) from other cities and towns around it. Boundaries might be natural features like rivers or man-made features like streets. Remember, a community is a group of populations living together in the same place.

   Record five boundaries of your community.

   a. _____ b. _____

   c. _____ d. _____

   e. _____

3. List some of the jobs that people perform in your community.

   a. _____ b. _____

   c. _____ d. _____

   e. _____ f. _____

4. Animals live in your community. List some animals that are found in your community.

   a. _____ b. _____ c. _____ d. _____

   List three animals that are not found in your community and tell why.

   a. _____ _____

   b. _____ _____

   c. _____ _____

5. Many different kinds of plants grow in your community. List some plants that are found in your community.

   a. _____ b. _____ c. _____ d. _____

   e. _____ f. _____ g. _____ h. _____

6. Make a list of four plants that do not grow in your community. Why can't they survive there?

a. _____   _____

b. _____   _____

c. _____   _____

d. _____   _____

Part II:

A large community can have smaller communities within the same boundaries. Look again at your map. Find four areas within your town that are smaller communities, and give each one a name. One of these smaller communities must be your own school area. List the four smaller communities.

a. _your school_   b. _____   c. _____   d. _____

Identify the boundaries of each smaller community.

a. _____   b. _____   c. _____   d. _____

1. _____   1. _____   1. _____   1. _____

2. _____   2. _____   2. _____   2. _____

3. _____   3. _____   3. _____   3. _____

4. _____   4. _____   4. _____   4. _____

List different animals that live in each small community.

a. _____   b. _____   c. _____   d. _____

1. _____   1. _____   1. _____   1. _____

2. _____   2. _____   2. _____   2. _____

3. _____   3. _____   3. _____   3. _____

4. _____   4. _____   4. _____   4. _____

List different plants that grow in each small community.

a. _____   b. _____   c. _____   d. _____

   1. _____   1. _____   1. _____   1. _____

   2. _____   2. _____   2. _____   2. _____

   3. _____   3. _____   3. _____   3. _____

   4. _____   4. _____   4. _____   4. _____

Part III:

Now that you have thought about the large and small parts of the community where you live, answer these questions with the information you have.

1. What is your definition of a community?

   _____

2. What is a population?

   _____

3. Are all the populations in your smaller communities the same or different? Explain your answer.

   _____

   _____

4. What do you think are the reasons that the populations of plants and animals are not the same in each part of the community?

   _____

   _____

   _____

5. What do you think will happen to a single population in a community if its food supply is taken away?

   _____

ACTIVITY

Understanding Conditions That Affect a Community

Introduction
Your students have all experienced the factors that affect their environment. The conditions that are necessary for a community to survive include proper temperature, water, soil, light, and an adequate food supply. This activity will focus the knowledge students have gained using their own observations of seasonal activity.

From the NSES—p. 157–158
See "Populations and Ecosystems."

Objective
The student will identify the factors affecting a community: temperature, water, soil, light, and an adequate food supply.

Materials
- Large sheets of newsprint (divided into 5 sections)
- Markers

Teacher Instructions
1. Divide the class into four groups. You should have 6 to 8 students in each group. Assign each group a season—summer, fall, winter, spring.
2. Each group should choose a secretary who will have the large newsprint and a marker. You can facilitate the activity if you prepare the newsprint with headings for the five columns as follows:

WEATHER CLIMATE	ANIMAL/BIRD POPULATIONS	PLANT POPULATIONS	HUMAN ACTIVITIES	OTHER

3. Tell group members to brainstorm alone for each of these areas, focusing on their own season and making notes on student worksheet 16.
4. When all students have finished the individual brainstorming, the secretary should record all information on the group chart and add any new ideas. Instruct the secretary to write in large letters, because the chart will be viewed by the entire class.
5. After 20 minutes, stop the activity, have all students face the front of the room, and have the secretaries bring up the charts to be taped on the chalkboard.

6. Student groups should summarize seasonal activities. Emphasis should be on a comparison of weather conditions during each season and the activity of plants and animals. (See Sample Chart 16.)

7. After each group finishes, ask the rest of the class to offer any additions.

8. You should then take over the discussion. (Note: an extended discussion of the following questions will take an additional class period.) Ask the following questions to direct the learning:

   a. Which season seems to have the most activity? Why? (Spring into early summer because of the warming temperature, longer days, and shorter nights.)

   b. What happens to the activities of plants, animals, and people as seasons change from summer to winter? Why do activities slow down? (Decreasing temperatures, decreasing food supply, and shorter days.)

   c. Why do some animals and birds leave a community in the fall? (Lack of food, lack of shelter, instinct.) Why do they return? (Hormonal changes, increasing food supply, increasing light.)

   d. What causes plant or animal activity to slow down as it gets colder? (Chemical change brought on by dropping temperatures.) How does that make a plant look? Where do the animals go? How do people protect themselves?

   e. What effect does rain or snow have on activities during a season? (Human activities may not occur, food-seeking behavior ceases, and animals "hole up.")

   f. What could happen if the conditions of the winter season were the same all year? (Limited or no plant growth, many animals would not survive, no food.) Would you like to live in that community? Could you?

   g. Has anyone in the class experienced a condition which drastically affected a community such as drought, severe storms, great amounts of rain or snow? What happened?

   h. If conditions in a community are bad, what will happen to that community? Why? (The necessary factors must be balanced for the community to survive.)

9. Return to the seasonal charts. How do the conditions such as temperature and light change the activity during a season? (For instance, if it gets too hot, animals hide, experience great thirst, and some die; plants wilt; water evaporates.) How would a community change if one of these factors were permanently altered? (If there was too much heat or no rain, the land would gradually become a desert; if flood conditions existed, the geography would be altered and the plant and animal populations would change.)

Other Ideas to Explore

1. Erosion of beaches because of seawalls
2. Loss of food supply due to overpopulation strains and drought (as in Africa and India)
3. Weather changes resulting from clear cutting of trees
4. Weather changes due to development of land
5. Erosion of soil because of poor farming practices

ACTIVITY

Sample Chart 16 Autumn				
Weather/climate	Animal/bird populations	Plant populations	Human activities	Other

cool
moist
snow flurries
rain
hurricanes
sleet
muddy
fog
Indian summer
	ducks/geese moving
	groundhogs fattening
	blue jays at feeder
	robins
	chipmunks gathering
	snakes/reptiles
	    and amphibians
	        hibernating soon
	deer active
	birds migrate
		colorful
		leaves falling
		asters/goldenrod
		last of the
		    garden
		nuts ripen
		many die
		needles falling
		ferns dry up
			hunting
			fishing
			Halloween
			back to school
			football games
			soccer
			wool sweaters
			storm windows
			    on the house
			clean up the
			    yard
			rake leaves
				daylight
				    decreases
				constellations
				    change

Understanding Conditions That Affect a Community

You will use the information you have observed about the seasons to discuss the effect these conditions have on the activity in a community. Your teacher will assign you to a group. Each group will analyze and discuss a particular season.

Your season _____

Weather/climate	Animal/bird populations	Plant populations	Human activities	Other

1. Brainstorm by yourself for information that would belong under each column in the chart above. Write a word or descriptive phrase explaining each of the parts of a community during your season.
2. Select a secretary for your group who will then make a master list of all the students' ideas in your group.
3. You will be comparing your season with the other three seasons in a full class discussion.

 ACTIVITY

Decision Making in a Community

Introduction

This activity describes a fictitious community with a recreational area threatened by development. It is an ecologically attractive area with a pond surrounded by forest. The pond is the water supply for the town, and residents have always been able to enjoy the benefits of the area.

You may use this activity as just a discussion activity or, if you wish, you may give your students a chance to apply what they have learned about ecological principles in a role-playing debate activity. In either case, the teacher instructions will be clearer if you read through student worksheet 17 first.

From the NSES—p. 46

Nurture collaboration among students.

Objective

The student will use ecological principles to solve problems presented in an imaginary situation.

Materials

- Student worksheet 17
- Pen or pencil
- Role cards, cut out, if you plan to have the students carry out a debate on this issue

Teacher Instructions

1. Begin this activity by handing out the student worksheet 17. Students should read the background information on the worksheet. You may wish to elaborate to make sure students clearly understand this activity's purpose. As an added activity, after students read the background, you may wish to have them make maps of the area. The maps would include all the features described in the background information—farms, the pond, the mountain, the streets of town, houses, directions to Less Perfect—and anything else they wish to add.
2. Have students answer the questions in Part I of student worksheet 17.
3. Discuss the students' answers to these questions. Clarify the financial as well as the ecological aspect of this problem.
4. Read aloud the situation in Part II of student worksheet 17. Students may respond to the discussion questions following the situation description. This is an especially good time to integrate the social political aspects that can destroy the ecological factors of a community and the part that money plays. You should include in your discussion groups that support laws to save wetlands (state or U.S. environmental protection agencies, Nature Conservancy, Audubon Society, and others). Emphasize what citizens can do to save land and living things.

5. If you are going to have the public hearing in Part III, you will need to assign each student a part by handing out specific cards to specific students. Assign major roles to students who can think on their feet. Give the students time to determine their roles and the attitudes they will be expressing. The background does not give students enough information, and you may wish to have them do some research on a particular aspect of the role they will play. This requires some time on the internet, a day in the library, a homework assignment, or possibly integration with social studies activities. For example, the role of the environmental protection agency representative—what approach does this state or federal agency take to the development of wetlands? Some students might research the town meeting forum that is used at most hearings. When do they let participants speak? How much time can be spent on one topic? What does the moderator do if an argument occurs?

6. You might culminate this activity by having a mock election to decide the fate of Perfect Pond. The students are the citizens of the village of Perfect. Ballots can be designed, lists of registered voters prepared, and ballot boxes constructed. The referendum would combine social studies with science.

Role-Playing Cards

You may wish to cut out and laminate these cards or reproduce them for each class's use. Consolidate or eliminate jobs to suit the class's size.

PRESIDENT Perfect Pond Hunting Association	CITIZEN #3 Perfect Town Employed in Less Perfect
GIRL SCOUT LEADER	FARMER #1 Vegetable
BOY SCOUT LEADER	FARMER #2 Dairy
TOWN MANAGER Perfect Town, USA	OWNER Perfect Town Construction Company
MR. BIG BUCKS Real Estate Developer	BANKER
ENVIRONMENTAL PROTECTION AGENCY-Representative	GEOLOGIST
PRESIDENT Perfect Pond Fishing Association	GAME WARDEN
OWNER Boat Rental Business	PRESIDENT Perfect Town Audubon Society
PRESIDENT Perfect Town Water Company	EDITOR, newspaper Perfect Town Journal
OWNER Perfect Town Sporting Goods Store	PRESIDENT Cool Can Company
CITIZEN # 1 Perfect Town	ELECTRICAL CONTRACTOR

CITIZEN #2 Perfect Town	WASTE DUMP OPERATOR
CHAIRMAN Zoning Board of Perfect Town	TOWN COUNCIL MEMBER 4
SUPERINTENDENT Perfect Town School System	TOWN COUNCIL MEMBER 5
TOWN COUNCIL MEMBER 1	POLICE CHIEF Perfect Town
TOWN COUNCIL MEMBER 2	FIRE CHIEF Perfect Town
TOWN COUNCIL MEMBER 3	ARCHITECT for Mr. Big Bucks
ATTORNEY for Perfect Town	ATTORNEY for Mr. Big Bucks
GOLF COURSE MANAGER	

Decision Making in a Community

Part 1. Background

Perfect Pond is located at the west end of Perfect Town, Anywhere, USA. It is a sparkling pond and is the water supply for the residents of Perfect Town. There are 500 acres of land surrounding the water with timber growth of maples, oaks, spruce, and pine. This pond was formed by glacial activity. The existing rock structure is granite and basalt. A glacial silt deposit covers the bottom of the pond and the shoreline. The runoff from nearby Pyramid Mountain feeds the pond.

A large variety of plant and animal populations have made this a successful community. Hunting and fishing regulations are strictly enforced.

The human population of Perfect Town uses Perfect Pond as a recreation area for boating and fishing. No swimming is allowed because this is also the town's water supply. Groups use campsites and picnic areas around the edge of the pond. There are hiking and skiing trails which can be used during all seasons.

Many of the residents of Perfect Town own large farms that produce vegetables, beef, pork, lamb, and dairy products. The younger generation commutes to the city of Less Perfect where they have jobs in factories and offices.

Questions to consider:

1. Identify the reasons the people of Perfect Town enjoy the area known as Perfect Pond.

   _____

   _____

2. Why would the citizens want to keep Perfect Pond as it is?

   _____

   _____

3. Are there any costs to the citizens of Perfect Town in keeping Perfect Pond as a recreation area?

   _____

   _____

National Science Teachers Association

4. Design a plan Perfect Town could use at Perfect Pond to make money and at the same time keep Perfect Pond as a recreational facility for the town.

_____

_____

_____

_____

5. List the positive and negative effects that might happen if the town followed your plan.

Positive (good)   Negative (bad)

_____   _____

_____   _____

_____   _____

_____   _____

6. Do you suggest that the citizens of Perfect Town follow your plan? Why or why not?

_____

_____

_____

_____

Part II. A New Situation Develops

The town manager of Perfect Town has received a proposal from Mr. Big Bucks to purchase the area at the west end of town known as Perfect Pond. The 200 acres on the eastern edge of the pond would become a housing development. The area closest to the lake would be for single-family houses. Behind the houses a condominium development would be built. It would be three stories high to offer a view of the pond. Ten acres would be developed into an 18-hole golf course.

The western edge of Perfect Pond would be sold to the Cool Canning Company. Cool Canning would buy local vegetable products and process them. This company would employ 100 people.

Name _____ Date _____

Questions to consider:

1. Should Perfect Town sell Perfect Pond to Mr. Big Bucks? Why or why not?

_____

_____

_____

_____

2. List the *positive* aspects of such a sale. What does Perfect Town gain if it accepts Big Bucks' plan?

POSITIVE: _____

_____

_____

_____

3. List the *negative* aspects of such a sale. What does Perfect Town lose if it accepts Big Bucks' plan?

NEGATIVE: _____

_____

_____

_____

4. Think of all the people who will be affected if Mr. Big Bucks is allowed to buy the real estate. List them, and note whether they will be affected positively

(P) or negatively (N). _____

_____

_____

_____

_____

National Science Teachers Association

Name _____ Date _____

5. How would Cool Canning Company help the community of Perfect Town?

   _____

   _____

6. What are some of the problems facing Perfect Town if Cool Canning builds a plant near the pond?

   _____

   _____

7. In what ways would this development plan change the ecology of the Perfect Pond area? _____

   _____

   _____

   _____

8. What laws does Perfect Town have that could prevent major changes if the town decides to sell the pond? (Assume that it is in your state.) For instance, are there any laws that prohibit dumping of wastes in the pond?

   _____

   _____

   _____

   _____

Part III. A Solution Develops

The Town Council has decided to have the people of Perfect Town vote on this proposal at the next election. A referendum requires public hearings to discuss the pros and cons of the problem. Some of the questions to be covered in the public hearing should include:

1. In what ways would this development plan change the ecology of the Perfect Pond area? _____

   _____

   _____

Name _____ Date_____

2. Does Perfect Town have any laws that could prevent major changes if the town decides to sell the pond? _____

_____

_____

Your teacher will organize your class to participate in this activity.

National Science Teachers Association

Surveying Small Communities

Introduction

Now you have introduced your students to the concept of a community, it is time to take them outside to explore small communities. You should select two areas of different conditions and populations. If you find that your school grounds cannot provide you with the communities, you can initiate the activity at school and have the class complete the activity at home. A home activity, however, will produce varied results, and students will have to work harder to achieve the same results.

You will need to review the meanings of the words community, population, and boundary. This activity will require that you have some knowledge of plant and animal names.

Objective

The student will survey a small community, identify its boundaries, and identify and count its populations. The conditions that control the community will be determined.

Materials

- Student worksheet 18
- Pen or pencil
- Folder or clipboard
- Jackets for students
- Whistle for student return signal

Teacher Instructions

1. You need to locate the two small communities and identify some of the plants and animals before going outside with your students. This will greatly facilitate your teaching. (Examples might be school lawn, athletic field, playground, a woods or stream near the school yard, or even a drainage ditch for run off water.)

2. You and your students will need to prepare for this activity a day ahead. If the weather indicates, students may need jackets or sweaters. Make sure all students have something to write on and pencils before going outside. Make sure there is adequate supervision of students, especially around potential hazards like deep water. Be sure to follow recommendations in "Health and Safety in the Field, p. 12."

3. Pass out student worksheet 18. Discuss the meaning of the word *community*. Review the concepts of boundaries and populations with your students. You may also wish to review the methods used to count populations. Remember, this is an initial activity. The more complex community survey technique, the line transect, follows. It is important for students to understand this simple activity first.

4. Have students record the name of each small community you plan to explore with them. This is most effective if the communities are as diverse as possible within the confines of your school grounds. If no significant diversity exists, you can use microhabitats—a crack in the sidewalk, a puddle, a tree, a dead log. A second alternative would be a field trip to a zoo, an aquarium, a greenhouse, an arboretum, or a natural history museum. The sole purpose should be to identify populations in a community. These places will provide varied habitats for your students' observations.

On the day of the activity:

1. Review rules for outside behavior, check to be sure everyone has materials needed, and have students prepare to go outside.

2. When you reach your first community, group students so that all can see the entire community. Having them sit or stand in a large circle is most effective for this. Proceed to identify the boundaries of the community as a group. Students should record those creatures on their worksheets and sketch the area on the back of the worksheet if they wish. (Refer to boundaries in Activity 15.)

3. Send students throughout this community to identify and count the animal populations. Tell them to observe carefully to locate all possible populations. Ants are underground, but we see ant hills; birds fly overhead; crawling insects may be found on buildings or tree trunks; squirrels may be in trees. In the appropriate column students list the populations found and record a population count. After about 10, minutes have students return to the circle and share the names and numbers of the animals they discovered. You may add any species missed. Students should record all species seen.

4. Repeat the same activity with the plant populations. You will have to guide the students on this part of the activity as the names of plants are not as familiar as animal names. Once they have identifed the plants, they can count the populations. This is an excellent opportunity to encourage observation of characteristics that distinguish species (size and number of needles, shape of leaves, color of bark, flowers). If no one knows the name of a plant or animal, describe it, draw it, or collect a sample to locate later in a field guide.

5. Take a few minutes, and have the group discuss the conditions of the community. These are the factors significant for the success of this community (See Activity 16).

6. Spend about 20 minutes in one community, then move to the other one and repeat steps 2 through 5 in this new community. Again, when specific identification is a problem, continue to encourage description, drawings, or collecting samples.

Surveying Small Communities:

Observations

Small Community Name	Populations (Animals)	Number	Populations (Plants)	Number
boundaries				
small community name				
boundaries				

Experimenting With Carrying Capacity and Overpopulation in a Grassland Community

Introduction
This experiment provides students with a view of the complex interrelationships in a community by illustrating the effects of overbreeding and variations in food supply. Outcomes will vary. You should attempt to identify the factors influencing outcomes. (For example, a grass crop may fail because students forget to water the plants, thus causing drought conditions.) This experiment is best done by a small group of students who share their results with the entire class. Information can be communicated by using a large chart on which daily data is recorded.

From the NSES—p. 168
When an area becomes overpopulated, the environment will become degraded due to the increased use of resources.

Objective
The student will be able to observe, describe, and alter conditions required for survival in a community. The student will be able to predict changes in one population based upon changes in the numbers of another population. The student will be able to explain the basic food chain concept.

Materials
- Container (30-liter aquarium would work) with a tight-fitting screen cover
- Gravel to scatter on the bottom of the container
- 3 to 4 inches of humus to cover the gravel
- Fast-growing grass seed
- Jar lid filled with wet sand
- Small toilet paper tube for crickets to hide in
- Dead branch for chameleons (anoles) to bask on
- Shallow dish with water
- Vegetable peelings
- Male and female crickets (Male cricket has two "tails"; female cricket has two "tails" and one thick, pointed ovipositor.)

Teacher Instructions
1. Prepare container with gravel and soil base, sprinkle thickly with grass seed, water frequently, and keep in sunlit window. Record daily checks of germinating dates and watering dates, using chart 19. Some fast-growing seeds will germinate in two to four days. Others take longer.

ACTIVITY

2. When grass cover crop is thick and healthy looking, add a few crickets and the small jar lid with wet sand. (Crickets lay their eggs in this medium.) Move the container so it gets indirect light or filtered sunlight.

3. Make daily recordings of changes in the grass cover and/or cricket population. Adult crickets have a life span of six to eight weeks, so the observation period could be anywhere from six to eight weeks. The nymphs look like adults and molt six to twelve times before reaching adulthood. Then they live six to eight weeks.

4. If the cricket and grass populations remain in balance, choose one of the following steps. In all cases, record daily changes in plant and animal populations. Continue to water to sustain plant growth.

   Step A. Add more crickets. Increase the cricket population artificially, and don't feed them. Is the grass crop an adequate food source?

   Step B. Add more crickets, and supplement their food with fresh fruit and vegetable scraps and peelings.

5. If the cricket and grass populations do not remain in balance (i.e., the crickets destroy the grass crop), the experiment is over and students should answer questions at the end of their worksheets.

6. If a balance is maintained with the students' help, alter the environment slightly by adding dead twigs, branches, and a rock or two. Add one green anole (an insectivore) to the container. Do not keep the container in direct sunlight. Observe carefully what happens to the cricket population.

7. The experiment may end naturally, or students may wish to keep the anole and crickets fed as classroom pets.

8. Discuss the experiment, and review the data chart and the results with the entire class. Answer the questions at the end of the worksheet.

Name _____ Date _____

Experimenting With Carrying Capacity and Overpopulation in a Grassland Community:

Instructions

A defined area can support only a certain number of individuals within a single population. This is called *carrying capacity*. When the population increases beyond that number, several things may happen. Members of that population begin to die more quickly, the food supply becomes depleted, some of the population may move away, or members of the population will adapt and learn to eat a different type of food.

You will be doing an experiment to determine the effects of cricket overbreeding on a community. The results of this experiment may be different each time you make and record your observations. Try to identify the factors influencing your results. For example, the grass crop may fail to grow because you did not give it enough water or because there are too many crickets living in the same area.

Part I. Setting Up the Experiment

1. Your teacher will provide you with the materials needed.

2. Take the container with the tight-fitting screen cover, fill the bottom of the container with gravel, and cover the gravel with 3 to 4 inches of humus.

3. Sprinkle the humus with grass seed (be generous, use plenty of grass seed). Place the container in a sunlit window, and water frequently. Begin at this point to record any changes you observe on Data Chart 19 under "Conditions of Grass." Be sure and note the date when you planted the seeds and began watering them and the date when the blades of grass can be seen.

4. Throughout this experiment you should continue to water the grass crop. Grass is one of the populations in your community.

5. When the grass crop is thick and healthy, go on to Part II.

Part II. Conducting the Experiment

6. Add a few crickets. Put wet sand is a small jar lid, and place the lid in the container. Crickets may lay eggs in the jar lid. Record the date and the number of crickets that you use in this part of the experiment on Data Chart 19.

7. Move the entire container to a spot where the sunlight is not direct. This is referred to as filtered sunlight, or indirect light.

8. Make daily checks, and carefully record any changes you observe in the grass cover and the cricket population.

9. If the cricket and grass populations remain in balance, choose one of the following steps. In all cases, continue to record any changes that you see in the plant and animal populations. Make sure you continue to water the grass so it will continue to grow.

   Step A. Add more crickets. You are now increasing the cricket population. Their food supply will be the grass. Do you think the grass crop will be enough food for the cricket population? Why or why not?

   Step B. Add more crickets and an anole. Supplement their food with fresh fruit, vegetable scraps, and peelings from any of these.

10. If you follow Step A and the cricket and grass populations do not remain in balance (i.e., the crickets destroy the grass crop), then your experiment is over. Answer the questions at the end of this worksheet.

11. If a balance is maintained as in Step B when you are also feeding the crickets, alter the environment slightly by adding dead twigs or branches and one green anole (an insectivore) to the container. Be careful not to keep the container in direct sunlight. Make daily observations on the condition of the cricket population. Answer the questions at the end of this worksheet.

12. You may end the experiment whenever you like. If you achieve a balanced carrying capacity, the crickets and anole could remain as classroom animals for observation all year.

Experimenting With Carrying Capacity and Overpopulation in a Grassland Community:

Questions

1. Describe the grass crop at the beginning of the experiment and at the end of the experiment.

    _____

    _____

2. How many crickets were living in the man-made environment and surviving in a healthy condition?

    _____

3. If you followed Step A, when did the cricket population become too large for the grass population?

    _____

4. If you followed Step B, did the inclusion of the anole alter the cricket population?

    _____

5. Write a hypothesis that would allow an experiment to be set up to prove what might happen if you added several anoles to the container. Set up the experiment and record the results. Was your hypothesis correct?

    _____

    _____

    _____

6. Draw conclusions about the carrying capacity of your grassland community. For crickets. For anoles. _____

    _____

    _____

    _____

    _____

Experimenting With Carrying Capacity and Overpopulation in a Grassland Community:

Data Chart 19

	Date	Intervention: What you did today	Condition of grass		Comments
Part I					
	Date	Intervention: What you did today	Condition of grass	Condition and number of crickets	Comments
Part II					

National Science Teachers Association

Line Transect:

A Classroom Demonstration of the Method for Surveying a Small Community

Introduction

The instructions in this activity are designed to help you preteach the major survey method your students will be using to examine communities at school and on the field trip. This activity will be new to most students, so demonstrating in class how to establish a line transect before you go outside will answer many questions. Instructions are included here.

The line transect method uses only a small section of any large natural area, yet produces an accurate representative sampling of the biotic and abiotic parts of a community. It is an exciting and stimulating activity, but does require a great deal of teacher preparation for it to be a success.

The time you spend preparing will make the results well worth your effort. Your students will spend several exciting days investigating and mapping their community using this method.

This activity is the introduction for your students, and it takes place in the classroom. Activity 21 takes students outside on school property to practice making a sample community survey.

From the NSES—p. 32

Encourage and model the skills of scientific inquiry, as well as curiosity, openness to new ideas and data, and skepticism that characterize science.

Objective

The student will be introduced to the purpose and function of a line transect, a method for obtaining a representational survey of a community.

Materials

- Line transect
- 20 meters of string on a handle with a nail on one end of the string and the other end attached to the wooden handle (instructions follow)
- Student worksheet 21
- Assorted plants and animals
- 1-meter stick
- Pen or pencil
- Plain white paper (one piece per student)

ACTIVITY

Preactivity Preparation

1. *Constructing the line transect.* Your technology department may be willing to make the handles for the line transect from scrap material, or you could use square blocks of wood and wrap the line around that. Buy heavy kite string for the line and 5-penny spikes for the anchor. Measure 20 meters of string and tie it to the wooden handle and wind up. Tie the spike to the other end. It is helpful, but not necessary, to identify the 5-, 10-, and 15-meter marks by using colored yarn or felt marker.

2. *Gathering plants and animals for classroom instruction.* A collection of the plants and animals—geraniums, gerbils, cacti, aloe vera, turtles, goldfish, spider plants—in the classroom can serve the purpose for this introductory lesson. If none is available or the variety is not adequate, cut pictures from magazines, glue them on sturdy paper, and attach feet at the base so the pictures will stand up along the line. At least 5 to 8 plants and the same number of animals will be adequate.

Teacher Instructions

What is a Line Transect? (Teacher Demonstration)

1. Hand out student worksheet 21 and a piece of plain paper to each student.
2. Have students read the worksheet, define line transect, and write a reason for using one.
3. Discuss the definition of line transect and relate that to the community study. What are the problems when you try to measure and count entire populations of a community? Refer to Activity 10. (Populations are too big, no way to keep track of mobile animals that have been counted.) The same results can be achieved by using a transect survey.
4. Setting up the line. Demonstrate as you talk.
   a. The nail is the 0-meter mark of the line transect. Outside it is pushed into the ground.
   b. Unroll the string. The handle end is the 20-meter mark.
   c. Place assorted plants and animals at intervals along the line. This demonstrates to students how the line is set up to use in a community survey.
5. Making a map of a community
   a. The papers students have will become the map of the community.
   b. Students draw a line across the middle of their papers and label 0, 5, 10, 15, 20 meters on the map to represent the line transect string.

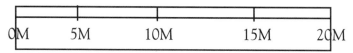

   c. All items along the line transect must be identified, measured, and counted and then mapped.
   d. Discuss various methods for identifying items with a symbol. Pictures, letters, or shortened words may be used. This is a chance for creativity.
   e. Do a sample transect with your students.

National Science Teachers Association

1) Go to the 0-meter mark on the line, identify the first population for the students. Locate the 0-meter spot on the students' papers, and label the population found there with an appropriate symbol. It is helpful to survey the entire line transect, first recording plant information (height should be measured in centimeters and recorded), and then returning to look for animal information.

2) Each plant population should be mapped at its appropriate position, identified, and measured.

3) After completing plants, go back and record animal information. Animals are not measured.

4) Check to make sure students have recorded all information you have given them.

5) Discuss the method with students, and make sure they understand the method for survey of any community.

6) Point out to your students that a major difference between this demonstration and the outside experience is that inside you are providing only a few plants and animals. Outside, across a grassy lawn, through a grove of trees, or over a vacant lot, the students will encounter hundreds of plants, insects, and possibly several animals.

7) Roll up the line transect.

Line Transect:

Using the Line Transect Method in the Field

Please read the instructions for Activity 20 before beginning this activity.

From the NSES—p. 123
Skills necessary to become independent inquirers of the natural world.

Objective
The student will use the line transect method to map the biotic factors (plant and animal populations) of a community.

Materials
- Line transects, one per student group
- Meter sticks, one per group
- 8 long pieces of surveyor's tape or brightly colored ribbon
- Plain white paper, one piece per student
- Clipboard or folder provided by each student
- Pencils
- Appropriate outside dress
- Optional whistle

Preactivity Preparation
1. Before you take your students outside, go out yourself and choose the community sites your students should survey. Identify each site with the surveyor's tape or ribbon. Tie it on a convenient branch at eye level. These are the points for the beginning of the surveys. Students will place nails in the ground at these points and roll the lines out to their full extents. Students will return to the tape markers each day.
2. Prepare the line transects. (See Activity 20.) You need one transect per group. The class should be divided into four groups, 5 to 7 students per group. Each group should select co-leaders to share organizational responsibilities. These groups will work together for the in-school activities as well as the major field trip. (See "Grouping," page 196.)
3. Collect meter sticks. Although rulers will work, meter sticks are easier to use.

Teacher Instructions (before leaving the classroom)
1. Assign students to groups. Go over health and safety concerns.
2. Pass out a line transect and meter stick to each group, pass out plain paper to each student, and make sure each student has a pencil and a clipboard.

3. Have students review the concept of the line transect method and how to lay out the line. Emphasize that the nail is the zero mark and that they should push it into the soil to hold the line. The handle is the 20-meter mark.

4. Have students draw the map line on their papers before going outside. They will record all plant and animal population information along this line. Recording this information may take students one to three class periods, 30 minutes per outside time, to complete.

5. Assign sites to each group.

6. Ask for questions.

7. Tell students the outside rules.

   a. Students must not run or shout.

   b. Emphasize that this is a science project and students have a task that must be completed.

   c. Students may not visit other groups under any circumstances.

   d. All members of the group must help with the work.

   e. One person must be responsible for each piece of equipment.

   f. Students must obey signals to return to starting point. (A whistle is helpful.)

Teaching Tips

1. The transect (survey site itself) is 20 meters long, 2 meters wide, and as high as the sky.

2. All populations within this space must be identified, counted and measured, and then recorded on the map. If students cannot identify a population immediately, encourage them to draw or write descriptions, or possibly collect a sample for field guide study when they have returned to the room.

3. The use of a legend is very effective. Symbols represent populations and are placed on the line at the proper mark. All members of the group must agree on the symbols used. (See Sample Line Transect A and Sample Line Transect B. In these samples, the legend is built into the line transect itself.)

4. Measure large populations by estimating. Count a specific area, then multiply by the number of areas being considered. Estimate tree height by holding a meter stick against the trunk and estimating the number of meters to the top of the tree.

5. Anything that flies or leaps across the line is counted—birds, insects, squirrels.

Sample Line Transect A

Grass

0	1	2	3	4	5	6	7	8	9	10	11	12	13	14	15	16	17	18	19	20

Indian paint-brush
Moss
Butter-cup
Wild strawberry

Patchy
6
5

Clover patchy
Dande-lion
White pine
Moss
Ferns

Dock
Golden-rod

Fly
Flea
Tiny black fly
Red spider
Ant
Ant
Flea
Ant
Leech
Black spider
Painted turtle
Water spider
Gray bug
Water spider
Mosquito
Black spider
Dragon-fly
Red spider
Green frog
Flea
Black ants
Leech
Flea
Black ants

Gray spider
Water beetle
Frogs
Water beetle
Water boat-man
Little leeches
Snail
Black spider

Sample Line Transect B

Animals		Plants
GRACKEL		
GREY SPIDER, FLIES, BUTTERFLY	— 0	GRASS, BUTTERCUP, MOSS, CLOVER
SPIDER		
TINY BLACK FLEA	—	BUTTERCUP, GRASS, WILD STRAWBERRY
ANT, RED SPIDER, FLEA	—	
ANT, FLEA	— 5	BUTTERCUP, WILD STRAW., CLOVER, GRASS, DANDELIONS
	—	DANDELION, CLOVER, FERNS
	—	DANDELION, GRASS, CLOVER, FERNS, WILD STRAWBERRIES, MOSS
	—	GRASS, MOSS
FLOATING	—	GRASS, HAY, MOSS
BLACK SPIDER, LEECH BUG		
WATER BOATMAN, PAINTED TURTLE, LEECH	—	HAY, MOSS, WATER LILIES
ORB SNAIL		
WATER BEATLE, FROG	— 10	GRASS, WEEDS, MOSS
LITTLE GREEN BUG	—	MOSS, GRASS, WEEDS
FROG, MOSQUITOES	—	GRASS
	—	GRASS, CLOVER
DRAGONFLY	—	GRASS, WEEDS, GOLDENROD, DOCK
MOSQUITOES, FROG	— 15	THISTLE, GRASS
RED SPIDER	—	THISTLE, GRASS
	—	GRASS
FLIES	—	GRASS, WEEDS
FLEA, BLACK ANT	—	GRASS, WEEDS
MOSQ., LEECH, GREEN BUG	— 20	GRASS, WEEDS

Line Transect:

A Method for Surveying a Small Community

The line transect is a method ecologists use to investigate any community. This method surveys a small section of a natural area. You will be able to locate, survey, and map the important parts of a community using the line transect method.

Define a line transect: _____

_____

_____

Explain the purpose of the line transect:_____

_____

_____

_____

    Your teacher will demonstrate how to set up and complete the map (the map is actually a cross-section drawing) of any community using the line transect method. You will practice recording information on your paper while your teacher demonstrates. All plants and animals should be located, identified, measured (plants only), and counted. Your completed map will provide a picture of the populations in a community.

Name _____ Date _____

Instructions for Outside

A. Identify and count plant populations
    1. Begin at the zero-meter mark (the point where the nail is in the ground). Identify plants along the first meter (and one meter to the sides) of the line.
    2. Record the information on the map. Use a symbol to identify each species. Don't forget to count and measure the size of each plant population and record this information.
    3. If the same species is found at other places along the transect, use the same symbol at each spot along the line.
    4. Continue until all of the plant populations have been identified, counted, and recorded.

B. Identify and count animal populations
    1. Repeat steps number 1 through 3 above, locating animals.
    2. Animal size is not measured.
    3. Look closely on tree trunks, dig under ground, and look carefully under logs or dead leaves for animals and insects.
    4. Birds, insects, and animals may be counted if they cross or fly over the line.
    5. Continue until all animals are named, counted, and recorded on the map.

Soil:

Living or Nonliving?

Topic: soil types
Go to: *www.scilinks.org*
Code: EXPL120

Introduction

In this experiment students will explore the makeup of soil. By removing the live creatures that make their homes in soil, the students can then examine the remaining debris to locate mineral materials (pieces of rock) and organic matter (dead leaves and plant litter).

From the NSES—p. 160

Soil consists of weathered rocks and decomposed organic material from dead plants, animals, and bacteria.

Objective

The student will be able to construct a Berlese funnel for the purpose of examining creatures living in soil. The student will be able to explain soil composition.

Materials

Each group of four students will need
- Soil from the forest floor (this may be collected in a plastic bag and should include an area about one-foot square, several inches deep)
- Funnels (dark colored so light will not penetrate; they could be made from aluminum foil)
- Large jars
- Rubbing alcohol
- "Bowls" made of 1/8 inch screening
- 75- or 100-watt lightbulbs in lamps
- Magnifying glasses
- White saucers
- White paper toweling
- Insect field guides would be helpful

Teacher Instructions

1. Divide the class into groups of four, and provide each group with the above materials. Each group will construct a Berlese funnel following the instructions in the student worksheet.
2. After the funnel has had a chance to work for a day or two, students should pour the alcohol and contents of the jar into a white saucer.
3. Students should then examine and identify the creatures in the saucer with the help of a magnifying glass and field guides and record their data on Chart 22A.

4. Students spread the remaining dried soil on the paper toweling. They should try to separate small pieces of gravel, clay, sand, sticks, leaves, and other debris and group them according to categories:

   a. organic matter, also called humus (such as leaves, twigs, and stems)

   b. mineral matter, particles of soil (such as clay, silt, sand, and large pieces of rock or stones)

5. Students take the two piles and, in each, attempt to find the smaller parts of the large mass (i.e., find the leaves [one pile], twigs [another pile], sandlike particles [another pile]). This isn't easy to do, but it should help them to look at the content of soil. Students should make a list of what they find.

6. Help them understand that if they put all this material back together again, they will have soil.

Name _____ Date _____

Soil:

Living or Nonliving?

In soil you will find a naturally occurring mixture of mineral matter, water, air, and other organic material such as dead plants. You will also find many creatures who live in the soil. In this activity, you will take apart a soil sample.

Part I. A Berlese Funnel

You will examine the living creatures in soil. The soil provides a home for a multitude of animal life forms. Some you will be able to see in this experiment. Most of the living organisms in your soil sample are microscopic—such as bacteria, fungi, algae, protozoa, and nematodes—and you will not be able to see them. You will be looking for different types of worms; grubs (they look like worms with legs); arachnids, or spiders; mites, or ticks (eight legs); insects (six legs); and snails. Earthworms are one of the most important groups of animals, because their presence indicates soil that is high in organic matter. In general, this animal group is responsible for converting the nutrients in undecayed organic matter to inorganic forms for growing plants to use.

Instructions

1. Your teacher will give your group the materials necessary to construct the Berlese funnel, which is a setup for extracting animals (mainly insects) from soil. Follow the directions and use the illustration to guide you.

2. Fit the bowl made of 1/8-inch wire screening into the funnel.

3. Put 1/4 inch of alcohol in the jar. If you want to keep your animals alive, omit the alcohol.

4. Place the funnel in the jar.

5. Put the soil sample into the screen bowl, and place the unit under the light source. The heat from the bulb will dry out the soil, forcing the small animal life such as worms, grubs, spiders, mites, millipedes, and other insects to burrow deeper into the moist parts of the soil. It will take 4 to 12 hours for the soil sample to dry. Eventually, these creatures will fall into the bottle of alcohol.

6. After a day or two, pour the alcohol and contents into a white saucer.

7. Examine and identify the creatures with the help of a magnifying glass and field guides.

8. Record your data of animal finds on Chart 22A. Share and compare your data with other groups. Consider the season in which you are doing this activity. Would you find more or less animal life at a different time of year?

_____

_____

_____

Chart 22A Animal Finds in Soil				
insects (6 legs)	arachnids (8 legs)	earthworms	grubs	snails

Part II. Soil—Organic and Mineral

In the second part of this experiment, you will separate the remaining parts of the soil that have dried in the screen bowl in the funnel into different piles or groups.

1. Put newspaper on your desk to hold all the soil pieces.

2. Dump the dried soil into one pile.

3. Separate the pile into the following groups.

Group 1—Organic matter, also called humus, such as leaves, twigs, stems, rotting wood, dead and decaying plants.

Name _____ Date _____

Group 2—Mineral matter, particles of soil, such as clay, silt, sand, and large pieces of rock or stones.

These mineral parts of soil are created by the natural processes of wind, water, temperature, and chemical forces acting upon rocks. Soil is being made all the time, every day.

4. Take each of the two large piles, and try to divide them into their components. For instance, in the organic pile do you find dead leaves? Put them in one pile. Twigs? Put them in another pile. Rotting wood?

    In the mineral pile, can you separate the pieces of stone from sand or loam?

    Make a list of what you find in your soil sample and record the data on Chart 22B. If you put this material back together again, what will you have?

Chart 22B Soil Composition	
Organic matter	Mineral matter

Naming Soils

Introduction

A simplified process that scientists use to classify soils is presented in this activity. Samples of the four basic soil types are described by their texture and then identified with a name. Soil texture is determined by the quantity of the particle size in a given soil sample. The larger the size of the particles, the closer the soil is to its rock origin. As the particles are broken down by the weathering process, they become smaller, changing from rock to gravel and then to sand. When sand particles mix with organic materials, silt and loam are formed.

Topic: soil types
Go to: *www.scilinks.org*
Code: EXPL120

From the NSES—p. 160

Soil consists of weathered rocks and decomposed organic material from dead plants, animals, and bacteria. Soils are often found in layers with each having a different chemical composition.

Objective

The student will describe the texture of soil samples and identify the four basic soil types: gravel, sand, loam, and clay.

Materials

- Student worksheet 23
- Soil samples of the 4 basic soil types
- 24 plastic or styrofoam cups
- Newspaper
- Pencil

Preactivity Preparation

Four soil samples must be available for the students to look at and feel. They must include gravel, sand, loam, and clay. Divide the 4 samples and place them in 4 separate styrofoarn cups. Prepare a soil set for each group of students. Label the cups "A" for gravel, "B" for sand, "C" for loam, and "D" for clay. Provide newspapers to protect desks.

Teacher Instructions

1. Distribute student worksheet 23. Have students read the introduction.
2. Divide the class into six groups, and hand out newspapers to protect desks. Distribute the prepared soil sample cups to each group.
3. Discuss the words *texture* and *particles* from the introduction.
4. Have students compare the soils by feeling, observing, and smelling them. For each sample they should write descriptive words on Data Table 23. The descriptive words on the student

worksheet are meant only to get them started. Encourage students to use their own vocabulary in addition to the words provided.

5. Discuss and compare the textures based on the sizes of the particles. (Gravel is very rough; loam and clay are smooth.)

6. Now have the students continue with the activity by reading further and using the information on Chart 23. Each soil sample can be named and the soil name recorded on Data Table 23 on the student worksheet.

7. Discuss the final paragraph. Students will identify soils in the field in Activity 24.

Naming Soils

Introduction
You can learn a great deal about soils by observing and feeling their texture. Texture refers to the quantity of different-sized particles you may find in a soil sample. Some of the following words might describe how the soil samples feel when you touch them: coarse, gritty, velvety, slippery, sticky, floury.

1. Look at, feel, and smell each soil sample your teacher has given your group. The samples are labeled A, B, C, and D.

2. Write the words which best describe the texture of each soil sample in the proper space in Data Table 23.

3. Perhaps you can think of other descriptive words to add to the list.

Data Table 23		
Sample	**Description of soil texture**	**Soil name**
A		
B		
C		
D		

4. Soils are divided into four large groups according to the quantity of different-sized particles found in an individual sample. Use Chart 23 to help you decide into which group the soil samples you are working with are classified and named.

5. Carefully observe each soil sample (A, B, C, and D).

6. Compare your observation to the information on Chart 23. Decide which type of soil you have.

7. Write the soil name on Data Table 23 beside its texture description.

Chart 23 Soil Type and Texture	
Soil type	**Soil texture**
gravel	coarse, many pebbles
sand	coarse, fine grains, no pebbles
loam	dark color, velvety, particles soft
clay	smooth, slimy, sticky when wet

You will notice that identifying soils is not as easy as it would seem. The particles may be combinations of two or more different textured soils. To solve the problem, soil scientists combine names to identify more correctly the sample. Examples include: sandy loam, clay loam, sandy silt loam. You may find several different types of soils in the same region. You may also find similar soil textures that are different colors. Clay may be gray in one area and brown or red just a few miles away. The color of a soil depends on the chemicals in the rock that produced the soil.

Classifying Soil Samples

Introduction

In carrying out this activity students will need to collect soil samples. If you are using the line transect community survey method, Activity 21, this is an ideal assignment. If not, students can gather soil samples by any method you desire, i.e., dig in the school yard, at home, a vacant lot, building sites. If there is no way students can provide their own samples, you could bring in samples for them to classify.

The easiest method for student classification is the "snake-roll" method. Even the youngest children have rolled clay snakes. The soils are classified by how closely the sample comes to forming the snake shape.

From the NSES—p. 160

Soils are found in layers with each having a different chemical composition and texture.

Objective

- Students will classify soil samples based on texture and the "snake-roll" test and will record the results.
- Materials
- Many plastic bags (ziplock are best) labeled 5 cm, 10 cm, 20 cm, and 30 cm (3 sets for each group)
- Implements for digging (trowel, camp shovel, spoons)
- Folder or clipboard to write on
- Pencil
- Student worksheet 24

Teacher Instructions

1. If students are responsible for providing the digging tools, you will need to remind them a day or two before the activity.
2. Begin this activity with a brief introduction to soil formation. Soils are formed when weathering (wind, water, freezing, and melting) act on a matrix (large rocks). This causes the matrix to break into smaller pieces. It takes thousands of years to change rock into soil. When you make a cut into the earth, the newest soils are usually on the top; the deeper you dig, the older the soils become. If you collect samples from each level, you can create a soil profile.
3. Students go outside for this activity. They collect samples at the line transect sites they used in Activity 21.
4. Follow student activity instructions numbers 1 through 8.
5. When you return to the classroom (or the next day), discuss the soil types and ask students to compare locations and soil classification.

Topic: soil types
Go to: www.scilinks.org
Code: EXPL120

6. Discuss the differences between soil types and their effect on plant growth. What makes loam? (Decayed plants and animals.) What plants will grow in sand? (Cacti.) Which plants won't? Why? (Any plant that requires a lot of moisture and doesn't have a method for storing water or preventing water loss.)

7. As a continuation of this activity, you may want to discuss and demonstrate a soil profile for the class. The following illustration is a typical soil profile. For further soil information, see the bibliography.

8. Any students who did not complete Activity 21 can participate in this activity if you provide soil samples.

Classifying Soil Samples

Soil is formed when large rocks are acted upon by outside forces like wind, precipitation, and temperature changes like freezing and melting. Large pieces of rock become smaller and smaller. It takes thousands of years to change rock into soil. Soils form layers or horizons. By collecting the soils from each horizon, you can form a soil profile. The newest soils are usually at the top layer of a site. The deeper you dig, the older the soil becomes. For this activity you will be working at your line transect site.

Instructions

1. Identify three different digging spots along your line transect.

2. At the first spot, dig to a depth of 5 cm, collect a soil sample, put it in a plastic bag, and label the bag.

3. Continue to dig to a depth of 10 cm, collect a soil sample, put it in a plastic bag, and label the bag.

4. Dig to a depth of 20 cm, collect a soil sample, put it in a plastic bag, and label the bag.

5. Dig to a depth of 30 cm, place a soil sample in a plastic bag, and label it.

6. Repeat steps 2 through 5 at the other two digging spots on your line transect

7. Classify your soil samples by performing the "snake-roll" test on each sample. Compare your results with classification Chart 24A below.

Chart 24A Soil Classification	
Soil type	**Snake-roll test**
gravel	will not roll
sand (tiny particles)	will not roll
loam	rolls, but breaks
clay	rolls and keeps shape well

8. Record the results of this test on Chart 24B.

Depth	Results of snake roll	Type of soil	Results of snake roll	Type of soil	Results of snake roll	Type of soil
Chart 24B Soil Classfication						
30 cm						
20 cm						
10 cm						
5 cm						

Answer these questions:

1. Compare the types of soils with the depth. How does the soil type change as you dig deeper?

2. What type of soils are best for plants? Why? Where do you find these soils—near the top of the soil profile or deeper?

Determining Soil Porosity

Introduction

Soil porosity refers to the interaction between water and soil types. The more porous the soil, the sooner water will drain through it. In most communities, a site evaluation is required to obtain a building permit. This is especially true in rural areas where sewage is handled through a septic tank system. When the water does not drain away readily, there is increased danger of major pollution and subsequent health problems. The interaction between water and soil types is especially pertinent in areas of estuary flow or when water supplies are affected.

This simple test will give students a rough idea about the rate of water drainage at a given test site.

Topic: soil types
Go to: *www.scilinks.org*
Code: EXPL120

From the NSES—p. 160

Water is a solvent. It dissolves minerals and gases and carries them to the oceans.

Objective

The student will determine and record the soil porosity for a given test site.

Materials

Materials are simple, but must be acquired before the activity. For each group of students have
- 1-liter plastic drink bottle with both ends removed
- 1-liter container, full of water with the top on tightly
- Timing device (Timing can be as rough as counting seconds, watches that tick off the seconds are better)

Teacher Instructions

1. Hand out student worksheet 25. Review directions with the class, and demonstrate the procedure for this test. (Use the student worksheet for your own information.)
2. This activity will be performed along the line transect from Activity 21.
3. Because students are working outside, it is important to reinforce rules for outdoor behavior (see Activity 21).
4. Students should complete student worksheet 25 as they perform the soil porosity test.
5. Students should answer the questions at the end of the worksheet. The questions and answers will be an excellent basis for a class discussion on the effect of groundwater pollution.

Student worksheet questions and answers:

1. Explain in your own words what soil porosity is. (Soil porosity is the interaction between water and soil types.)

2. Name some types of plants that will survive in areas where there is little or no water available. (Cacti.) How are they able to do this? (Modified leaves so water does not evaporate, deep taproots, or many surface roots that cover a large area.) Name the type of community or larger ecosystem where these plants live. (Desert.)

3. There are types of plants that can live totally in water. Name a few. (Algae, seaweeds, pond lilies.) What do you call the type of community or larger ecosystem in which they live? (Pond, lake, ocean.)

4. Most plants require a balance between the desert and the pond. Why do you think that is so? (Most plants need adequate water. Too much water suffocates them; too little water causes wilting.)

5. Why are plants important to people and animals? (They are sources of food and oxygen.) Why are plants important to this planet? (They are sources of food and oxygen; they are recyclers of carbon dioxide; they provide beauty, products for human beings to use, and organic material for the soil.)

6. What will happen to the plants in an area if a flood or drought occurs? (They will be damaged, die, suffer stunted growth, or be destroyed.)

7. What effect might a building have on the soil porosity? (Compress the soil particles so water won't drain off the land.)

8. How or why does an area that drains slowly become polluted? (Microbial growth occurs in standing water.)

9. What effect does pollution have on plant and animal populations? (It makes water unusable; the pollution— for example, DDT, mercury poisoning in fish, or acid rain—is transferred to plants and animals and is carried on through the food chain.)

10. Describe the method you used to find the soil porosity of your ecosystem. Is it possible that one ecosystem might have different soil porosities? (Yes.)

Determining Soil Porosity

The test you will be making gives you an idea of the amount of moisture the soil you are working with can hold. It will also tell you how quickly the moisture will leave the ground.

Plants do need moisture to live, but too much water is just as bad for them as too little. Too much moisture prevents air from moving in the soil, and the plants will suffocate.

The rate at which water leaves a site is very important. Standing water may become polluted. This is especially serious when that water supply drains into another body of water. All communities require a test of some kind when new buildings are about to be constructed.

Part I. Conducting Your Experiment

1. Make sure your group has all of the materials it needs. Those materials include a plastic bottle, a gallon of water, and a timing device. If no timing device is available, you can get an adequate time by counting the seconds.

2. You will need to do the test three times. Make sure you do not use all your water on the first test. Decide how much is about 1/3 of the gallon.

3. Remember, you are doing an experiment. Pay careful attention to the results because you will be expected to make some decisions based on the results of this experiment.

4. When you reach your test site, select a location for the first test. Assign one person to be the timekeeper.

5. Put the plastic bottle down on the site. Twist it a couple of times to make sure it doesn't tip over. You may have someone in the group hold the can to steady it.

6. Pour 1/3 of the water from your jug into the plastic bottle. The timekeeper for your group should start the clock or begin counting as soon as you stop pouring the water. The counting should continue until all the water disappears into the soil. Record the results of the experiment in the space on Chart 25 labeled "TEST 1."

7. Move the plastic bottle to the second location. Repeat step 6. Record the data in the space on the chart labeled "TEST 2."

8. Move the plastic bottle to the third location. Repeat step 6. Record the data in the space on the chart labeled "TEST 3."

Name _____ Date _____

Chart 25 Soil Porosity	
TEST 1 _____	seconds for the water to drain
TEST 2 _____	seconds for the water to drain
TEST 3 _____	seconds for the water to drain

Part II. Interpreting Your Results

The faster the water drains out of the can, the more porous the soil. Porous soil can hold a lot of water before puddles will form. The more slowly the water leaves the can, the less porous the soil. Most plants do not grow as well in less porous soil. Fill in the chart below, and then answer the following questions about soil porosity.

TEST 1 We think the soil is:

_____ very porous   _____ porous

_____ slightly porous   _____ not porous

TEST 2 We think the soil is:

_____ very porous   _____ porous

_____ slightly porous   _____ not porous

TEST 3 We think the soil is:

_____ very porous   _____ porous

_____ slightly porous   _____ not porous

1. Explain in your own words what soil porosity is. _____

    _____

    _____

2. Name some types of plants that will survive in areas where there is little or no water available. How are they able to do this? Name the type of community or larger ecosystem where these plants live._____

    _____

    _____

    _____

National Science Teachers Association

Name _____ Date _____

3. There are types of plants that can live totally in water. Name a few. What do you call this type of community or larger ecosystem? _____

   _____

   _____

4. Most plants require a balance between the desert and the pond. Why do you think that is so? _____

   _____

   _____

5. Why are plants important to people and animals? Why are plants important to this planet? _____

   _____

   _____

6. What will happen to the plants in an area if a flood or drought occurs?

   _____

   _____

7. What effect might a building have on the soil porosity?

   _____

   _____

8. How or why does an area that drains slowly become polluted?

   _____

   _____

9. What effect does pollution have on plant and animal populations?

   _____

   _____

10. Describe the method you used to find out what the soil porosity of your ecosystem was. Is it possible that different ecosystems might have different soil porosities?

_____

_____

_____

Temperature Influences on a Community

Introduction

The amount of heat in an ecosystem is another of the abiotic factors that determine success or failure of that ecosystem. Plant and animal survival is directly linked to heating and cooling over a period of time. This task focuses directly on the temperature in a designated area on a given day. The students will be asked to graph the temperatures at measured intervals above and below the ground. You may use the results of their investigations to discuss the effects of heating and cooling of the environment. This is a basic introduction to the greater concept of climatic changes.

From the NSES—p. 122

Employ simple equipment and tools to gather data and extend the senses.

Objective

The student will measure and graph the temperature of the assigned site.

Materials

- Student worksheet 26
- Pen or pencil
- Folder or clipboard
- One each of the following per group:
    - Soil thermometer*
    - Meter stick or ruler
    - Timing device
    - Digging implement

* If soil thermometers are not available, small lab thermometers can be used. They break easily, and students need to use a great deal of caution to not get cut if the glass breaks. Using a thermometer that contains mercury is prohibited. If any of this type of thermometer are still in your supply closet, dispose of them according to regulations. Mercury is a carcinogen.

Teacher Instructions

Part I. Gathering Data
1. Hand out student worksheet 26.
2. This is a continuing activity for the line transect from Activity 21.
3. Check to be sure each student group has the necessary equipment.
4. Preview worksheet with students so that all instructions are clear. Note these important areas:

a. Where and how to place thermometers. CAUTION: Thermometers are easily broken. Students must take great care not to jam them into the ground or bang them against anything.

b. How and where to record data on Data Table 26.

5. Review outside rules of behavior, and reinforce task commitment. Take students outside.

Part II. Graphing and Analyzing Data

6. When you return to the classroom, demonstrate the method for plotting data on Graph 26. Some students won't need too much help; others will find this difficult.

7. Circulate in the class as students complete graphs for both locations I and II. Using a different-colored pen for each location helps emphasize the different locales.

8. If you think students cannot prepare their own graphs on the worksheet, you can make a graph worksheet for them. Older students should not have a problem with this part of the activity.

Part III. Drawing Conclusions

9. Students should use the data they have collected to complete the answers to the questions in Part III of their worksheets. The questions and possible answers follow.

a. What happened to the temperature as you moved above the ground? (It decreased.)

b. What happened to the temperature as you went deeper into the earth? (It was warm at the surface if the Sun was out; heat is absorbed by the soil, but the temperature cools further from the surface.) Predict the temperature at your site if you were to dig much deeper. (As you approach the center of Earth, the temperature cools and then becomes hot as you near the core.)

c. Compare the temperatures out in the open to those under bushes and trees. (Usually it is cooler under plants, warmer in the open.)

d. How is shade useful to animals? (It provides coolness for cold-blooded animals who could die in hot sun; it also provides respite for warmblooded animals on hot days.)

e. Why do leaves of plants face the Sun? (Leaves do not consciously face the Sun, but mechanisms have developed that allow them to turn in that manner to absorb the Sun's energy to carry on photosynthesis, the process of food making in plants.)

f. Why do people like to have plants around their houses? (Plants provide protection, keep drastic temperature changes from occurring, and provide beauty.)

g. Do you think temperature is an important factor in a community? (Living things require energy from the Sun. The by-product of this energy is heat. Plants and animals transform the energy into useful materials for a successful community.)

Temperature Influences on a Community

You will be taking the temperature of your ecosystem. After you record the data, you will plot the information on a graph.

Part I. Gathering Data

1. Your teacher will supply your group with the worksheet, a thermometer, meter stick, timing device, and a digging implement. You will need a pencil or pen and a clipboard or folder to write on. CAUTION: Handle the thermometers with great care; they break easily.

2. When you get to your assigned site, locate a position where you will begin. Lay the thermometer on the ground for 1 minute. Record the temperature on Data Table 26.

3. Measure 50 cm above the ground. Hold the thermometer at that spot for one minute. Record the reading on Data Table 26.

4. Repeat step 3 at 100 cm above the ground, and record the data on Data Table 26.

5. Dig a hole 2 cm deep at Location I. Carefully place the thermometer in the hole, wait one minute, and record the results on Data Table 26. CAUTION: Read the thermometer before you take it out of the hole.

6. Increase the depth of the hole to 5 cm. Repeat step 5, and record the data.

7. Dig to 10 cm, and repeat step 5.

8. When you are finished, replace the dirt in the hole.

9. Before you leave Location I, take the temperature in a few unusual places. For instance, you could measure the temperature under bushes or flowers, under thick shrubbery, in the water puddles, or any place that is a bit different. The thermometer should remain in place for one minute. Record all results on Data Table 26.

10. Now move to a second location at your site. It is more interesting to select a location that is quite different from the first spot.

11. Repeat steps 2 through 8 in Location II. Be sure to record all data on Data Table 26.

Part II. Graphing Data

1. Using the information from Data Table 26, find the temperature recorded on the ground at Location I.

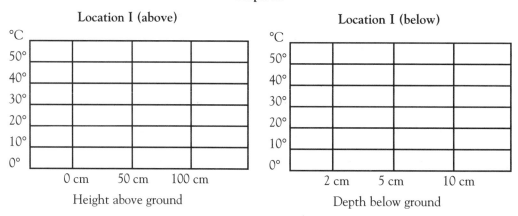

Name _____ Date _____

2. Place a dot at the correct point on Graph 26, Location I, which shows the temperature you recorded.
3. Complete both graphs from the information you recorded on Data Table 26 at Location I.
4. Now make your own graphs for Location II just like the graphs above. Complete the graphs for Location II using the information from Data Table 26.

Temperature Data Table 26			
Location I		Location II	
	Temp °C		Temp °C
on ground		on ground	
50 cm above		50 cm above	
100 cm above		100 cm above	
2 cm below		2 cm below	
5 cm below		5 cm below	
10 cm below		10 cm below	
under bushes		under bushes	
under trees		under trees	
other		other	

Graph 26

Location I (above)

°C
50°
40°
30°
20°
10°
0°
  0 cm   50 cm   100 cm
Height above ground

Location I (below)

°C
50°
40°
30°
20°
10°
0°
  2 cm   5 cm   10 cm
Depth below ground

Part III. Drawing Conclusions

Answer these questions based on this experiment and what you already know about plants and animals.

What happened to the temperature as you moved above the ground?

_____

_____

a. Predict the temperature at your site at 150 cm above the ground. _____
   at 200 cm above _____ at 250 cm above _____

b. What happened to the temperature as you went deeper into the earth? Predict
   the temperature at your site if you were to dig much deeper.

   _____

   _____

   _____

c. Compare the temperatures out in the open to those under bushes and trees.
   What causes the differences?

   _____

   _____

d. How is shade useful to animals?

   _____

   _____

e. Why do leaves of plants face the Sun?

   _____

   _____

f. Why do people like to have plants around their houses?

   _____

   _____

g. Is temperature an important factor in a community? Explain your answer.

   _____

   _____

ACTIVITY

Analyzing a Community

Introduction
The worksheet for this activity is designed to be used as a concluding activity in conjunction with Student Activity 21, "Line Transect: A Method for Surveying a Community."

Objective
The student will analyze data obtained from a community survey and apply it to new circumstances.

Materials
- Student worksheet 27
- Pen or pencil

Teacher Instructions
1. Review with students the definition of the words: community, populations (for plants and animals), and food web.
2. Review with students the concept of a successful community. A brief discussion of the biotic and abiotic factors which make a community a success will be helpful.
3. Students should complete their worksheets using the information they obtained in Activity 21. *Alternate Plan:* If your students have not done a community survey, you might have them design a community. They could draw a picture of it, identify the plants and animals, show the numbers of populations, and identify those conditions which make their "designed" community a success: proper amounts of water (rainfall), adequate temperature, proper quality of the soil, and interactions between the populations (food for all). You could use this activity to promote a class discussion about a successful community.

Analyzing a Community

1. Plan a way to show the location of the community you have surveyed. This can be in the form of a map or drawing on a separate sheet of paper. Make sure you identify the boundaries.

2. List the names of the plants you identified in your survey.

   _____

   _____

3. List the names of the animals you were able to identify in your community.

   _____

   _____

   _____

4. Name the two most abundant plants in your transect section. Describe the biotic factors allowing those plants to exist in such large numbers in your community.

   _____

   _____

   _____

   Do you find these plants in areas outside your transect section? Why or why not?

   _____

Name _____ Date _____

5. Were there a lot of animals along your transect? What kinds were the most abundant? The least abundant? Why? _____

_____

_____

_____

What conditions does this particular community provide so that the animals can live there? _____

_____

_____

6. Identify the types of soil you found along the line transect. Did the soil change as you dug deeper? _____

_____

_____

7. What can the study of soil layers tell you about the age of your community?

_____

_____

8. What factors make this community a success? _____

_____

_____

9. List three changes (natural or man-made) that might destroy the community.

a. _____

b. _____

c. _____

Name _____ Date _____

10. Pick one of the changes from your list. Write a paragraph that describes the appearance of your community if this change really took place. _____

_____

_____

_____

_____

11. Draw a before-and-after-the-change picture of your community on a separate sheet of paper.

12. Could your change have been prevented? If "yes," how could it have been prevented? If "no," why not? _____

_____

_____

_____

13. Think about: What would happen to the Earth if your change happened everywhere on the planet at the same time?

_____

_____

_____

_____

_____

_____

_____

PART 4

Food Web and Energy Flow

Concept Definitions

A food web is a network in a natural community of many species that have the ability to eat different kinds of food. The study of a food web must involve the study of producers, consumers, and decomposers and how they affect each other. Energy flow is the process by which some energy from the Sun is passed from one living thing to another in the form of food. Most energy from the Sun is not used and leaves the Earth, re-entering the atmosphere.

Topic: atmosphere
Go to: *www.scilinks.org*
Code: EXPL149

Objectives

The student will be able to
1. define and construct an energy pyramid
2. create a food web and identify the interdependencies within that habitat
3. identify and illustrate parts of the water cycle, the carbon-oxygen cycle, and the nitrogen cycle
4. demonstrate active knowledge of conservation measures

Process Skills

- Classifying
- Observing
- Communicating
- Collecting and analyzing data
- Drawing conclusions
- Making generalizations
- Measuring
- Predicting
- Inferring

These National Science Education Content Standards are addressed in this section:

Content Standard C

Food webs identify the relationships among producers, consumers, and decomposers in an ecosystem.

Plants and some microorganisms are producers—they make their own food. All animals including humans are consumers that obtain food by eating other organisms. Decomposers, primarily bacteria and fungi, are consumers that use waste materials and dead organisms for food.

For ecosystems the major source of energy is sunlight. Energy entering ecosystems as sunlight is transferred by producers into chemical energy through photosynthesis. That energy then passes from organism to organism in food webs.

Content Standard D

Water, which covers the majority of the earth's surface, circulates through the crust, oceans, and atmosphere in what is known as the "water cycle." Water evaporates from the earth's surface, rises, and cools as it moves to higher elevations, condenses as rain or snow, and falls to the surface where it collects in lakes.

The earth is a system containing essentially a fixed amount of each stable chemical atom or element. Each element can exist in several chemical reservoirs. Each element on earth moves among reservoirs in the solid earth, oceans. Atmosphere and organisms as part of the geochemical cycles.

Movement of matter between reservoirs is driven by the earth's internal and external sources of energy. These movements are often accompanied by a change in the physical and chemical properties of matter. Carbon, for example, occurs in carbonate rocks as limestone, in the atmosphere as carbon dioxide, gas, in water as dissolved carbon dioxide, and in all organisms as complex molecules that control the chemistry of life.

Content Standard F

Important personal and social decisions are made based on perceptions of benefits and risks.

Building an Energy Pyramid Vocabulary

Introduction

To fully understand associations within a community, you should introduce the relationships among organisms using food and energy.

An energy pyramid is defined as energy moving from the Sun, sustaining life on this planet, used by plants and animals, passed on, and lost to the atmosphere. An energy pyramid is made up of producers, organisms that make their own food, and consumers, animals that cannot make their own food and must eat plants and other animals. This activity will provide students with the opportunity to identify the vocabulary of the components of an energy pyramid and then to apply that information by constructing an energy pyramid.

From the NSES—p. 158

For ecosystems the major source of energy is sunlight. Energy entering ecosystems as sunlight is transferred by producers into chemical energy through photosynthesis. That energy passes from organism to organism in a food web.

Objective

The student will identify and define the parts of an energy pyramid and construct a diagram showing the positions of these parts in a typical energy pyramid.

Materials

- Student Worksheet 28
- Pen or pencil
- Trade books or texts to locate meanings of words
- Scissors
- Glue
- Construction paper

Teacher Instructions

1. Distribute student worksheet 28. Students will use available texts, trade books, or dictionaries to find the meanings of the words on their worksheets. Encourage them to put the meaning into their own words.
2. Students should follow the instructions on student worksheet 28.
3. Discuss the position, outside the pyramid, of decomposers, scavengers, and the Sun. Have students draw arrows indicating the transfer of energy from decomposers, scavengers, and the Sun to the energy pyramid.

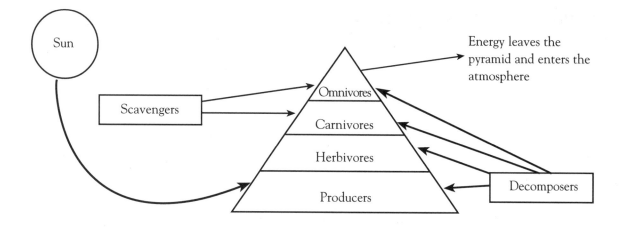

Definitions for Energy Pyramid
- Scavenger: an animal that feeds on dead animals; a consumer.
- Decomposer: a microbe that causes the decay or breakdown of dead plants and animals.
- Sun: the star that gives our planet light and heat necessary in the process of photosynthesis.
- Omnivore: an animal that consumes both plant and animal materials.
- Carnivore: an animal that eats other animals.
- Herbivore: an animal that eats only plants.
- Producer: any organism that makes its own food.

4. As an extension of this activity, solicit ideas from your students as to specific plants and/or animals that would fit at each level of the energy pyramid. You could draw these suggestions on the chalkboard, providing an introduction to the next activities. (Activities 29 and 30 provide more specific information about these concepts.)

Building an Energy Pyramid Vocabulary

Using the shapes on the next page

1. Find the meaning of each word in the shapes on your worksheet using a textbook or some other reference material. Write the meaning of the word inside the shape.

2. Cut out each shape. Make sure you understand the meaning of each word within the shape.

3. By using the meanings of the words and the information you already know, form a triangle showing the position of each group in a food chain in a community. (Clue: Not all of the shapes will be part of the triangle.)

4. After your teacher has checked your choices, glue your triangle on a separate piece of paper.

5. Glue the Sun in the upper left-hand corner of your diagram. Use arrows to show how the Sun's energy affects parts of the energy pyramid.

6. On the right side of the triangle, glue the decomposer. Draw arrows to show the parts of the pyramid these organisms affect.

7. On the left side of your diagram, glue the scavenger. Again draw arrows to define the parts of an energy pyramid affected by scavengers.

Name _____ Date _____

Scavenger

Decomposer

Sun

Omnivore

Carnivore

Herbivore

Producer

Constructing a Food Web I

Introduction

This activity is designed to give students a visual idea of a food web. A food web is defined as a complex interdependence within a community. These interdependencies determine the success or failure of the community in combination with the abiotic factors (weather, water, temperature, light, and soil conditions) and adequate food supply. The plants and animals in a given habitat depend on all of these factors. If one or more of them is altered, the populations have three choices: change habitat (move), adapt to the new conditions, or die.

This activity will focus on the interdependencies developed among the plants, animals, and the Sun to create food webs. A brief description and visual example of the intended product is helpful.

Objective

The student will create a food web and identify the interdependencies within the habitat.

Materials

- Large supply of magazine pictures of plants and animals (cut up *National Geographic*, *Ranger Rick*, *Audubon*, *Natural History*, *National Wildlife*, or other regional nature and wildlife magazines)
- Large sheets of newsprint (36" x 24")
- Markers or crayons
- Pencils or pens
- Reference books such as encyclopedias or field guides
- Student worksheet 29

Preactivity Preparation

To accumulate a collection of pictures of plants and animals, go through nature magazines and remove photos of wildlife. Students can do this for you as a leisure-time activity. Plan for 6 to 10 pictures for each group of students. It is helpful to have a food web bulletin board (see Part I, "Management, Mechanics, and Miscellany") so students can see what a food web diagram looks like. You can use the bulletin board as a teaching tool many times during this unit.

Teacher Instructions

1. Organize students into small groups of about 3 to 6. You may use groups that already exist, have students choose their own groups, or assign groups.

2. Hand out student worksheet 29, a large piece of newsprint, and crayons or markers.

3. Give 10 or more pictures to each group, or have a large pile of pictures available. One member from each group should select pictures.

4. Tell students to follow directions 1, 2, and 3 on their worksheets.

5. When student have questions about what a particular animal eats, have them look for answers in field guides or encyclopedias.

6. Your responsibility is to check the progress of groups, but not to provide direct answers.

7. When a group believes it has an accurate food web, you should approve it. Then the students recreate the web by gluing the pictures to the newsprint, adding other parts of the community (Sun, water sources, trees). If there are not enough pictures available, students may draw on the newsprint the food web they have arranged. See the sample food web on the next page.

8. After the food webs are complete and labeled (step 4 on student worksheet 29), students should draw arrows that show the food supply of each member of the habitat. Be sure the web includes the materials necessary for plants to carry on photosynthesis, such as Sun, water, soil nutrients.

9. Students should identify their community/habitat based on the type of plants and animals that live there.

10. Students answer question 8 on their worksheets. Answers should be in complete sentences.

Alternate plan: Provide 1 set of food web pictures on a bulletin board or poster. Students would start the activity with step 2 on student worksheet 29 (connect plants and animals to their food supply). The rest of the directions can be accomplished either by groups or individuals. The finished product should be approximately the same.

Sample Food Web

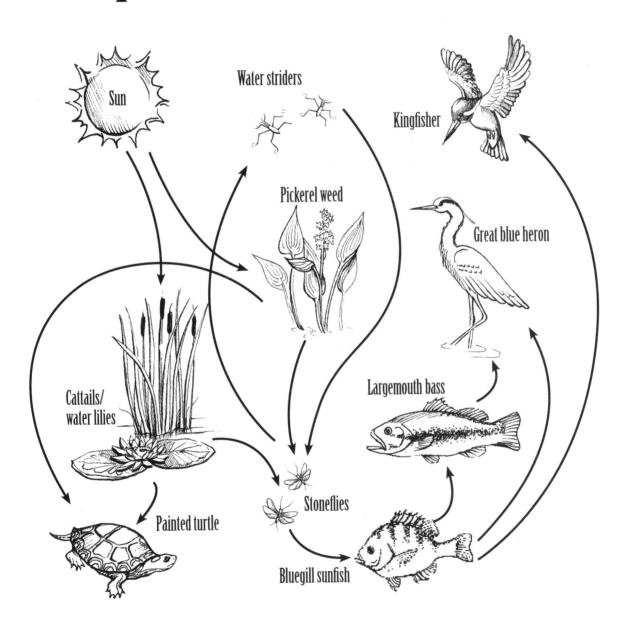

Sun

Water striders

Kingfisher

Pickerel weed

Great blue heron

Cattails/
water lilies

Largemouth bass

Painted turtle

Stoneflies

Bluegill sunfish

This is a pond food web.

Constructing a Food Web I

Food webs are a complex interdependence within a community that involves many species with the ability to eat a number of different kinds of food. If a plant or animal is not able to satisfy its needs within its habitat, it has three choices. The plant or animal can

- move—change habitat
- adapt—adjust its life style to the new conditions
- die

1. You will be working in a group. Your teacher will provide your group with some pictures of plant and animals that would normally be found in the same place.

2. Organize your pictures so you can see connections between predators and prey. For example, frogs eat insects, insects eat plants. Arrange and rearrange all the pictures on a desk until you can provide each plant and animal with a food supply.

3. If the proper connection is not available in your picture pile, trade with other groups or draw the missing part of the food web.

4. On the large piece of paper, arrange your pictures to form a food web. It should have at least 5 or 6 animals and their food supplies. Label each picture. Draw arrows showing the connection between a plant or animal and its food supply.

5. Remember to include the ingredients that allow plants to make their own food supply (Sun, air—especially carbon dioxide, soil nutrients, and water)

6. Identify the type of habitat your group has created.

7. A food chain is a simple relationship of plants and animals within a food web. Be sure you can identify one food chain within your food web.
    Answer these four questions using complete sentences:

    a. What would happen if the Sun were no longer shining?

    _____

    _____

b. What would happen if the groundwater became polluted?

_____

_____

c. What would happen if there were no rainfall for six months?

_____

_____

d. What would happen if there were a large increase in one of the populations?

_____

_____

 ACTIVITY

Constructing a Food Web II

Introduction
This activity, fun and somewhat complex, will magnify for students the interconnections among all forms of life and the problems that can arise when one destructive action occurs.

From the NSES—p. 129
Organisms can survive only in environments where their needs can be met. When the environment changes some plants and animals survive and reproduce. Others die or move to a new location.

Objective
The student will explain the working arrangements of a food web, discuss what happens to the food web when pollution of some kind occurs, and consider options for protecting the environment against such damage.

Materials
- 5 balls of yarn (one of each color—yellow that will not be cut, and red, green, black, and brown, from which you will cut several 6-foot lengths)
- Scissors
- A piece of paper for each student identifying the role he or she will play (lists to photocopy follow the instructions)
- Safety pins or masking tape

Teacher Instructions
1. Review with the students the definitions of producers, consumers, herbivores, carnivores, omnivores, scavengers, and decomposers. (See Activity 28.)
2. Students should be divided into four groups representing four ecosystems—pond, ocean, field, and forest.
3. Groups should gather in four corners of the room. You will need to move desks so that eventually the groups can be connected. This is a great activity to do outside on a lawn or in a field. Ask students to sit down.
4. Give each student a card with the name of an animal, plant, or insect on it. Pin or tape the name on each student's shirt. The teacher, or another student, should take the role of the Sun.
5. Ask students to consider what type of organism they represent. For instance, "grass" would be a producer, "whirligig beetle" would be a carnivore, "raccoon" would be an omnivore, which is both a herbivore and a carnivore. Within each of the four ecosystems, students should decide who eats whom.

6. Once students have determined their roles within the ecosystem (the teacher's guide will help you with any questions that arise), ask all herbivores to raise their hands. Give each of these students a 6-foot piece of green yarn. Then ask carnivores to raise their hands and give each one a 6-foot piece of red yarn. If a student is both herbivore and carnivore, give red yarn and green yarn. Scavengers receive black yarn; decomposers receive brown yarn. Producers just wait for the Sun's energy.

7. The Sun will hold the yellow yarn. When all ecosystems are ready, i.e., all students know their parts and have their yarn, the Sun passes the yellow yarn (while retaining hold of one end) to the lowest level in the food web—any one of the plants. That plant passes the yarn on to another plant. (Point out that the Sun's energy comes directly to all plants, but for our purpose, the Sun will pass only one strand of yellow.)

   The yellow yarn continues to pass from plant to plant and on to the next ecosystem until the yellow Sun's energy has traveled to all producers. Let the end of the yarn just drop, and point out that most of the Sun's energy is not used and leaves the Earth, reentering the atmosphere.

8. Now ask the herbivores (green) within each ecosystem to decide whom they will eat. They should hold on to their yarn in the middle and tie each end of it to two plants in their system. Carnivores (red) will repeat the same procedure, tying to two animals. Omnivores have four possibilities as they have red and green yarn. Scavengers and decomposers may tie onto any plant or animal provided that they realize their meal has been rotting or dead for some time.

9. Once the connections within an ecosystem are complete (webbed), the complexity of food relationships in one place should be evident

10. If your students seem ready, begin now to ask questions that will stimulate thinking about relationships between ecosystems. For example: Does the deer ever leave the forest and go to the meadow? Does the gull leave the ocean and fly inland over the meadow? Does the raccoon eat clams at the ocean as well as bird eggs near the pond?

11. Once this movement is clear, to show the interconnections between ecosystems, give the deer in the forest another piece of long green yarn and ask him to also tie into the wheat grass in the meadow. Give the raccoon another piece of red yarn, and ask him to tie to the clam at the ocean. Give the herring gull black yarn, and ask him to tie to the meadow vole (dead). Many more of these connections can be made, but this is probably adequate to show the complicated arrangement of food in our world.

12. If you wish to carry this activity further, introduce a catastrophe at this point. For instance, tell students that an oil truck delivering heating oil to a farmhouse near the meadow has an accident resulting in a major oil spill. The oil runs off across the meadow and into the stream that feeds into the nearby pond. Ask all the animals and plants that will be affected by this event to drop their ties, in other words, make a break in the food web.

   If the meadow is coated with oil, most plants and animals will die. The runoff to the stream will affect some of the pond community. If the grass in the meadow dies, that will affect the deer in the forest, and so on. Continue this discussion as far as you wish to take it. You could invent another catastrophe such as pollution from a landfill also affecting water resources or air pollution from a factory affecting plant growth. Students should come away from this activity with a much clearer picture of food webs.

Roles to Play for the Food Web Construction Activity

Photocopy and cut out the blocks for the students' role-playing activity.

Pond	Meadow	Forest	Ocean (rocky shore)
algae	millipede	mushroom	herring gull
duckweed	aphid	earthworm	soft-shelled clam
bacteria	honeybee	wood thrush	periwinkles
mayfly nymph	wild strawberry	blackfly	ribbon worm
green frog	wheat grass	ruffed grouse	rockweed (fucus)

Pond	Meadow	Forest	Ocean (rocky shore)
bluewinged teal	Queen Anne's lace	red baneberry	spartina grass
raccoon	green snake	oak tree	great blue heron
golden shiner (fish)	red-tailed hawk	deer	beach flea
painted turtle	meadow vole	beech tree	shrimp
red-winged blackbird	earthworm	gray fox	rock crab

 ACTIVITY

Teacher Guide for the Food Web Roles

Pond
algae—producer
duckweed—producer
bacteria—decomposer
mayfly nymph—herbivore (eats water plants)
green frog—carnivore
blue-winged teal—primarily herbivore; occasionally carnivore (eats some insects)
raccoon—omnivore
golden shiner (fish)—omnivore (algae/small crustaceans)
painted turtles—young turtles are carnivores; old turtles are herbivores
red-winged blackbird—herbivore/carnivore (seeds/insects)

Meadow
millipede—herbivore (eats decomposing vegetation)
aphid—herbivore
honeybee—herbivore
wild strawberry—producer
wheat grass—producer
Queen Anne's lace—producer
green snake—carnivore (eats spiders and insects)
meadow vole—primarily herbivore (but eats some insects)
red-tailed hawk—carnivore
earthworm—scavenger

Forest
mushroom—decomposer
earthworm—scavenger
wood thrush—primarily herbivore (but eats some insects)
blackfly—carnivore
ruffed grouse—primarily herbivore (but eats some insects)
red baneberry—producer
oak tree—producer
deer—herbivore
beech tree—-producer
gray fox—omnivore

National Science Teachers Association

Ocean (rocky shore)

herring gull—scavenger

soft-shelled clam—omnivore (eats plankton)

periwinkle—herbivore (eats algae)

ribbon worm—carnivore

rockweed (fucus)—producer

great blue heron—carnivore

beach flea—scavenger

spartina grass—producer

shrimp—herbivore

rock crab—scavenger

Diagraming Your Own Energy Pyramid

Introduction
By studying plants and animals in other communities, students usually are not aware that they as well are consumers in a food chain or energy pyramid. This activity asks the students to examine the foods they eat and thus look at their position as a link in an energy pyramid.

Objective
The students will identify and list foods they consume and then identify each item as a link in an energy pyramid. The students will construct an energy pyramid with this information showing the food and human relationships.

Materials
- Student worksheet 31
- Pen or pencil
- Ruler

Teacher Instructions
1. Distribute student worksheet 31. Review with students the parts of an energy pyramid. See Activity 28.
2. Students should discuss their positions as consumers (omnivore, carnivore, herbivore).
3. Students should then follow the directions on their worksheets. You might have to help them determine what some foods actually are since they have been processed (i.e., bread comes from wheat).
4. Most students will be at the top of the energy pyramid. Some students are only vegetarians; therefore, those pyramids may not have items at each level.
5. You might wish to take this activity further and have students construct a food web for themselves. This could be used as an art activity as well.

Name _____ Date _____

Diagraming Your Own Energy Pyramid

You have already discussed the parts of an energy pyramid. In this activity, you will think about the food you eat. You will create a food chain that includes you and your own menu.

1. Choose your favorite meal. Write the name of each food you ate on a separate line in Chart 31. Make sure you include all the items from your menu. Complete only the menu column.

Chart 31 Your Energy Pyramid	
Menu	Food chain link
Item 1.	
2.	
3.	
4.	
5.	
6.	
7.	
8.	
9.	
10.	

2. Review these parts of the energy pyramid.

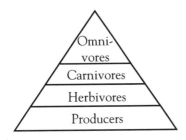

3. Look at each item on your food list and decide which type of link it represents.

  For example: Bread is made from wheat, a plant = a producer

  Hamburger is meat, a cow = an herbivore

  Return to Chart 31, and complete the food-chain-link column.

4. Draw a triangle on the back of your worksheet. Put the name of each food item in its proper section of the triangle.

5. Does your list contain any scavengers or decomposers? Which are they?

  _____

  _____

6. Which is the omnivore?_____

  _____

7. Don't forget the Sun.

8. Try this activity with another meal you ate. Do you have any empty spaces in your triangle? What does that signify?

  _____

  _____

Mother Nature's Recycling Project:

The Water Cycle

Introduction

Any study of energy flow in a community cannot be complete without discussing the replacement of natural resources necessary for maintaining life activities.

Because these four cycles are interdependent, it will be necessary to discuss each by itself and then unite all the information. Students need to focus on the interactions in order to understand the complexity of planetary needs.

Topic: water cycle
Go to: *www.scilinks.org*
Code: EXPL169

From the NSES—p. 160

Water, which covers the majority of the Earth's surface, circulates through the crust, oceans, and atmosphere in what is known as the "water cycle." Water evaporates from the Earth's surface, rises and cools as it moves to higher elevation, condenses as rain or snow, and falls to the surface where it collects in lakes, oceans, soil, and in rocks underground.

Objective

The student will observe and explain the parts of the water cycle.

Materials

- Drawing of the water cycle from student worksheet 32
- Clear 1-gallon jar
- 1 cup warm water
- 12 ice cubes
- 1 piece of clear plastic wrap
- A heat source (sunlight or a gooseneck lamp)
- Optional: a terrarium or aquarium

Teacher Instructions

1. Introduce this lesson by asking students to tell about an event they have participated in that involved water (swimming, boating, water slides, hoses, baths, selling Kool-Aid, rain showers) or snow and ice (skating, skiing, sledding, snowball fights).
2. Then discuss as a group the question: Where does the Earth get water? (Water comes from evaporation from lakes and oceans that falls as precipitation.)
3. Continue the discussion. If we keep using the water in a lake, how does it fill up again? (Lakes fill up from rain and runoff from land.)

4. Why does it rain? (While students are thinking about this, distribute student worksheet 32 which includes a diagram of the water cycle. The worksheet contains a skeletal outline on which students can take notes for future reference.)

5. You may begin explanation of this cycle anywhere. The most common point of origin is with a body of water. At this juncture, discuss with students the behavior of water molecules when they are heated and cooled. (When heated, molecules move more rapidly, bump into each other, and rise; when cooled, they slow down and move closer together.)

6. Ask your students to observe the illustration of the water cycle on student worksheet 32. Identify with students the part of the diagram that would directly affect the movement of the water molecules. (The Sun.) Where do the molecules that rise go? (Into the atmosphere.)

7. This movement of molecules rising into the atmosphere is called evaporation. Students should label the arrow leading from the water to the cloud with the word *evaporation*. Some students may know that water also enters the atmosphere from a process called transpiration in green plants.

8. The next phase to be discussed is condensation. The cloud is the significant object. (It should be labeled.) (As water vapor rises, it is cooled. When these molecules cool, they contract. Many of these droplets condense and form clouds.)

9. Ask students: Why does it rain? (As more and more droplets condense, clouds become heavier with water. Depending on the conditions between the atmosphere and the Earth's surface, the molecules fall back to the Earth as precipitation—rain, snow, sleet, hail.) Students should label the arrow from the cloud to the water with the word *precipitation*.

10. To demonstrate the water cycle, set up this water system.

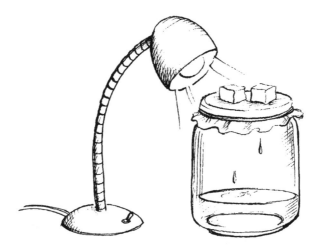

11. Using a terrarium or aquarium, discuss the continuous water supply in a closed ecosystem. Condensation on the glass demonstrates the temperature difference between the water or land surface and the top of the aquarium or terrarium.

Teacher Sample

The Water Cycle—Model Notes

I.   Need for water
    A. (Answers will vary.)
    B.
    C.
II. The Water Cycle
    A. Evaporation
       1. Water molecules are heated by the Sun.
       2. Molecules bounce around, move rapidly—some go into the atmosphere.
       3. Some water goes into the atmosphere because of transpiration from plants.
    B. Condensation
       1. As they rise, water molecules are cooled because the temperature decreases.
       2. They condense to form clouds.
       3. As clouds become full, they become heavy with moisture.

C. Precipitation
1. The type of precipitation depends on the atmosphere conditions.
2. There are four forms of precipitation:
a. rain
b. snow
c. sleet
d. hail
III. Conclusion
(Use this as a chance for students to summarize.)

Name _____ Date _____

Mother Nature's Recycling Project:
The Water Cycle

For plants and animals to stay alive, they must have water. This activity will help you understand how our planet continues to obtain water for all living things. Your teacher will discuss and demonstrate the water cycle. Use the following illustration to make sure you understand the three parts of this process. If you want to write down this information, use the outline form.

The Water Cycle

I. Need for Water

    A. _____

    B. _____

    C. _____

II. The Water Cycle

   A. Evaporation

      1. _____

      2. _____

      3. _____

   B. Condensation

      1. _____

      2. _____

      3. _____

   C. Precipitation

      1. _____

      2. _____

      3. _____

         a. _____

         b. _____

         c. _____

         d. _____

III. Conclusion

Mother Nature's Recycling Project:
The Carbon and Oxygen Cycles

Introduction

Green plants in your community will provide the basis for an understanding of how carbon, oxygen, and their compounds are produced and then recycled through the biosphere.

SC*L*INKS.
THE WORLD'S A CLICK AWAY

Topic: carbon cycle
Go to: *www.scilinks.org*
Code: EXPL175

Objective

The student will discuss and be able to explain the importance of the carbon and oxygen cycles.

Materials

* Student worksheet 33
* Pen or pencil
* Optional: an outside site where students can observe these processes occurring, or a classroom terrarium

Teacher Instructions

1. Ask students: Why must successful communities have green plants? (Plants are attractive, provide shade, food for animals and people, products, homes for animals and people, and release oxygen.)
2. Ask this favorite question: Where does a tree get its food? Have you ever seen a tree at the grocery store buying hamburgers and buns? Why not? (Plants are able to make their own food. To reinforce this idea, suggest planting one of the students outside for two weeks, feet firmly buried in soil, without any food, only sun and rain. What would happen to the student?)
3. Ask: What raw materials and energy sources are necessary for plants to make food? (Sunlight, chlorophyll, water, and carbon dioxide.)
4. Distribute student worksheet 33 which includes a diagram of the carbon dioxide-oxygen cycle. Have students use the illustration on the worksheet to observe the process of photosynthesis. Use the following information in your discussion of the carbon dioxide and oxygen cycles.
   a. Where is chlorophyll located in a green plant? (Leaves.)
   b. How does a green plant get light? (From our star, the Sun, or an artificial light source.)
   c. How does a plant get water? (From the soil through its roots; refer to the water cycle, Activity 32.)
   d. Where does the carbon dioxide come from? (Carbon dioxide comes from the atmosphere. Part of the natural makeup of the atmosphere is carbon dioxide; some of it is recycled in human and animal respiration.)

5. Summary and formula of the process of the carbon dioxide and oxygen cycles.

    The Sun's energy is trapped by the chlorophyll in the leaves of the plant. Carbon dioxide enters the plant through the stoma (openings) on the underside of the plants' leaves. Molecules of water and carbon dioxide are chemically rearranged to form a food product called sugar. Oxygen is released from the leaves into the atmosphere as a byproduct of the food-making process which is called photosynthesis. ($12 H_2O + 6 O_2 + light \rightarrow C_6H_{12}O_6 + 6 O_2 + 6 H_2O$).

    a. What does a plant do with the food it makes? (It uses the energy to continue its life processes: to grow, reproduce, and move.)

    b. Are there any other organisms that use the food produced by plants? (Some animals must eat plants because they cannot make food; other animals eat animals that eat plants.)

    c. How do animals use the oxygen that plants release into the atmosphere? (Animals need oxygen to change or oxidize food to release energy.)

    d. How do plants themselves contribute to the production of these substances? (When plants drop their leaves, they provide the basic materials that replenish some minerals for soil production. Microbes are necessary to break down these particles for plants to reuse.)

6. Discuss the relationship between water, carbon dioxide, and oxygen in the production and recycling of natural products. (Plants and animals depend on each other to supply necessary energy for life processes.)

Teacher Sample 33

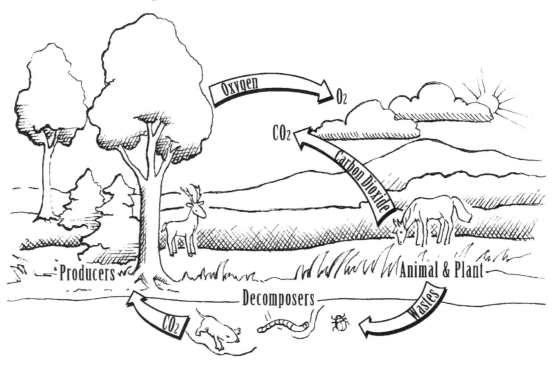

Name _____ Date _____

Mother Nature's Recycling Project:
The Carbon and Oxygen Cycles

A successful community provides the natural ingredients needed to support life. Two of the most important ingredients are carbon dioxide and oxygen.

By understanding how green plants make their food, you will get a better idea of how animals depend on plants. The results of the interactions between plants and animals provide those elements that maintain life activity.

Your teacher will ask questions that will make these ideas clearer to you. Look carefully at the following illustration. Make sure you understand all the parts of these cycles. Label the parts the teacher identifies for you.

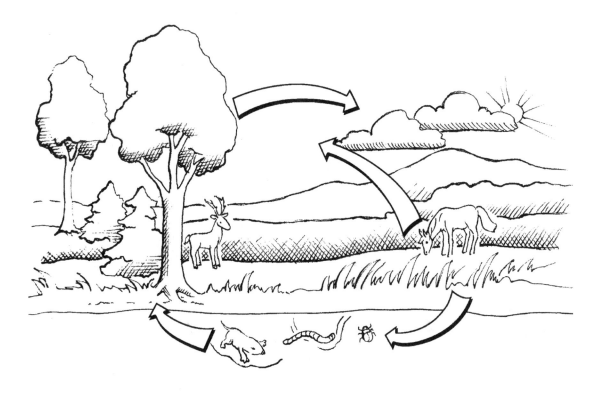

Mother Nature's Recycling Project:

The Nitrogen Cycle

Topic: nitrogen cycle
Go to: *www.scilinks.org*
Code: EXPL178

Introduction

Eighty percent of our atmosphere is nitrogen. Plants require nitrogen but are not able to utilize atmospheric nitrogen. They must absorb nitrates, nitrogen-containing compounds, dissolved in water from the soil. The processes that change organic substances into nitrates that can then be used by plants are illustrated in this activity. Again, there is a strong interrelationship among the biotic factors in the environment. It is especially important that you stress the concept that none of these cycles (water, carbon, oxygen, and nitrogen) is isolated, but instead that all of them work together in nature. Nothing is wasted or lost.

From the NSES—p. 189

The Earth is a system containing a fixed amount of each stable chemical or element. Each element can exist in several different chemical reservoirs. Each element on Earth moves among reservoirs in the solid earth, ocean, atmosphere, and organisms as part of the geochemical cycles.

Objective

The student will identify and discuss the parts and function of the nitrogen cycle.

Materials

- Student worksheet 34
- Pen or pencil

Teacher Instructions

1. Ask students to identify the gases that form our atmosphere. (Oxygen and nitrogen are the two major ones; others include carbon dioxide, hydrogen, helium, water vapor, and some trace gases.)
2. Which gas is the most abundant in our atmosphere? (Students invariably answer oxygen; however, the answer is nitrogen, which makes up about 78% of the atmosphere, with oxygen only 21%.)
3. Distribute student worksheet 34. Have students read the background information. You may wish to have them take notes, and a skeleton outline is provided.
4. Define the words *element* and *compound*. (Element—a substance composed of one kind of atom. Examples include oxygen, gold, and copper. Compound—a substance composed of two or more elements, chemically united in definite proportions. Examples include salt, sugar, and water.)

5. Name some of the elements and compounds we have already talked about in recycling in nature. (Elements include oxygen and carbon. Compounds include water, sugar, and carbon dioxide.)

6. To grow properly, plants must have the element nitrogen. Ask students: From your reading, what would the simplest way be for plants to get the nitrogen they need? (It seems from the atmosphere, the same way they get carbon dioxide. But plants are not able to use the nitrogen in the atmosphere. They can absorb only nitrogen dissolved in water through their roots.)

7. To explain that unusual situation, ask students to tell what happens to trees in the autumn. (Leaves fall off, and sugar and starch [food] are stored in roots.) Do the leaves pile up each year and stay in the same shape and form? (No, leaves are decomposed by microbes that change their chemistry.)

8. What happens when an animal dies? (Bacteria act on the remains, changing the proteins in animals and plants into nitrates. The nitrates are deposited in the soil. Decomposed animal wastes also provide nitrogen.)

9. There is one group of plants, the legumes (peanuts, beans, peas, clover), that have nitrogen-fixing bacteria living in tiny spaces in their roots. These bacteria are capable of taking the nitrogen from the air in the soil and storing it in a form that plants can use.

10. Farmers have long known that alternating non-nitrogen-fixing crops with some of the legumes produces better plant growth. You might wish to discuss the use of fertilizers that provide. plants with nitrogen when legumes are not grown.

Teacher Sample 34

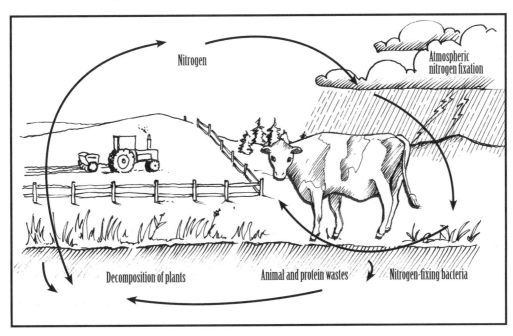

The Nitrogen Cycle: Model Notes

I. Need for nitrogen by plants
   A. Required to live
   B. Required to grow

II. Availability of nitrogen
   A. About 80% of the air is nitrogen. This cannot be used by plants.
   B. Plants must absorb nitrogen compounds through their roots.

III. Process of changing remains to nitrogen
   A. Microbes act on plants and animal remains.
   B. Proteins are changed to nitrates.
   C. Nitrates become part of the soil.
   D. Nitrates are absorbed by plants through their root systems.

IV. Nitrogen-fixing bacteria
   A. Live in tiny spaces in roots of legumes (e.g., peas and beans)
   B. Take nitrogen from the air
   C. Are stored in a form plants can use

V. Fertilizers provide nitrogen.
   A. Crop rotation using legumes helps crops.
   B. Adding fertilizer to soils that are nitrogen-depleted is necessary.

Name _____ Date _____

Mother Nature's Recycling Project:

The Nitrogen Cycle

Materials that plants and animals need to live and grow must be provided in their environment. Plants and animals depend on each other to change substances into the necessary elements and compounds.

One of the elements green plants must have to grow properly is nitrogen. Nitrogen is abundant in our atmosphere (almost 80%). The problem is that most plants are not able to use this nitrogen in the air but must absorb nitrates, nitrogen-containing compounds, dissolved in water through their roots.

Microbes (bacteria) act on the remains of plants and animals, changing proteins into nitrates. These nitrates are left in the soil and are absorbed by water. When water enters the plant through the root system, the needed nitrogen is available for plant growth.

The Nitrogen Cycle

I. Need for nitrogen by plants

    A. _____

    B. _____

II. Availability of nitrogen

    A. _____

    B. _____

III. Process of changing remains to nitrogen

    A. _____

    B. _____

    C. _____

    D. _____

IV. Nitrogen-fixing bacteria

    A. _____

    B. _____

    C. _____

    D. _____

V. Fertilizers provide nitrogen

    A. _____

    B. _____

A Recycling Project

Introduction

Most towns and cities must recycle part of their wastes. Landfills and trash disposal areas have become overloaded so quickly with our "throwaway" society's habits that an environmental crisis is occurring. This project demonstrates for students the absolute need for recycling. From both an economic and environmental standpoint, recycling makes sense. If the planet is to survive in good condition, students must take part in preserving it.

Topic: recycling
Go to: *www.scilinks.org*
Code: EXPL183

From the NSES—p. 168

Human activities also can induce hazards through resource acquisitions, urban growth, land use decisions, and waste disposal. Such activities can accelerate many natural changes.

Objective

The student will participate in a recycling project to better understand the need for and the meaning of the word *recycling*.

Materials

- Large trash bags (one for each day of the project)
- Scale to weigh recycled paper each day
- A large storage space

Teacher Instructions

1. Day 1. Introduce the word *recycle* (to use something over and over again). Discuss the problems towns and cities are experiencing with disposable waste. (Too much waste, it does not decompose fast enough, space is limited, and waste causes pollution.) One method towns and cities are using to solve this problem is to save certain trash items (cans, bottles, jars, and paper) and sell these items to companies that can convert them into useful products.

   Check with a local recycling agency to determine what type of paper is acceptable and how it should be bundled. Have students clean out their desks or notebooks and stack up any paper no longer useful to them. Put all of the paper in one trash bag. Weigh the paper by having a student weigh himself alone, weigh himself with the bag of paper, and subtract the difference. Record date and weight of paper on the board or on a chart you make and keep for the duration of this experiment.

2. Day 2. Repeat Day 1 with students. You will not get as much paper, so begin to encourage them to save paper so it can be recycled in science class and weighed.

3. Day 3. Continue to recycle and weigh paper each day. Some students will ask if they can bring in old papers from home; others will begin to suggest that they could clean out their

ACTIVITY

lockers and bring the paper to class; on occasion, other teachers will take part in the project too, and bring their paper to you. The only caution is to be sure that only clean paper is recycled. Leftover lunches are not part of the project!

4. At the end of the ecology unit, compile the total weight of the paper, making use of math skills.

5. Plan a trip to a local recycling plant, and select some students to help you deliver the paper for recycling. Use this opportunity to announce in school the amount of paper recycled that would otherwise have added to the landfill or disposal problem. This is a chance for good public relations between the school and community. The local newspaper may be interested in the story.

SECTION III

The Field Trip: Applying Ecology Concepts

Overview

Taking students on a field trip will be the most exciting event of the school year if you plan it carefully. Ideally, a field trip will provide the one opportunity for students to individualize their activities. The general class information they have gained—counting populations, sampling soil, surveying the line transects—will now have specific applications in a specific place unique to each group of children. A field trip allows for creativity, individual discovery and expression, and the extension of the classroom beyond four walls.

On a field trip students have the opportunity to handle parts of an environment and to eventually discuss man's position in a food web, pollution of that web and life sources, the changing role of nature, and the interdependence of all life. Much can be learned from text and trade books; more can be learned from being in the field.

Field trips are excitement generators. For the apathetic student, a field trip provides the occasion to work in a totally new environment. For all students, field trips are an opportunity to trust themselves and thoroughly enjoy learning.

Serious field trips follow serious classroom preparation. This text emphasizes active ecology study, not simply reading about or looking at one's environment. A field trip must have specific goals with definite tasks assigned. It is important to set these goals in conjunction with your students. Plan together.

The information students will be gathering will be used to prepare a presentation, a final collaborative activity done by each "site" group within a classroom. Make sure your students realize that extensive information gathered in the field will enhance their presentations in the classroom.

The activities in Section II prepared students for individual research in the field. The field trip's success will be directly related to the amount of careful teaching and planning that occurred before the field trip.

IMPORTANT: Before taking students into the field, reread the "Health and Safety in the Field," p. 12, and be sure to follow its recommendations for planning and execution.

Field Trip:

Site Selection, Preliminary Arrangements, and Discipline

Site

Site selection is crucial to the success of field trip day, but it need not be a search for exotic locations. A farm meadow, a city park, a riverside, an overgrown vacant lot—all may serve as sites for field work.

The number of sites selected will depend on

1. the size of the site—can it accommodate 10 or 50 children?
2. the safety aspects of the site—are there dangers or distractions in the immediate area?
3. the number of children you will be taking—100 students do better at four sites than one.
4. the number of buses and chaperones available—each group of 50 students needs at least two teachers and four or more parent volunteers.

Note: Each small group within the site (you may have eight class groups working at one site) should have one adult with it for guidance and supervision. Parents can be very helpful in this role even if they are not trained in outdoor work.

Preliminary Arrangements

1. You must get permission from the landowner to visit property. (Take along trash bags, and pick up everything when you leave.)
2. You must have a permission slip for each student. Students must have parental approval to leave school grounds and travel on the bus. Your school may already have a field trip permission slip form. A suggestion is shown below.

Sample Field Trip Permission Slip

Please sign the attached field trip permission slip:

_____ has my permission to participate in the

_____ grade field trip on _____ to the

_____ .

I know my child will be traveling by school bus to and from the site.

Date _____ Signature _____

3. If you are researching on public property, such as a city park, you may need special permission to do some of the experiments, soil sampling, for example.
4. Bus arrangements must be made through your school's transportation department. If you plan to do most of the activities suggested during the field trip, plan to spend four hours on site (lunch included).
5. Locate bathroom facilities. You may need to be prepared for sites without bathrooms. (We discourage heavy consumption of water before leaving school.)
6. Plan arrangements for handicapped students. A field or meadow site is more accessible for a student in a wheelchair.

Discipline

Repeat general discipline rules several times.
1. Behavior. Students are on private (or public) property. This is not home. No destruction of the area will be tolerated. No racing, wrestling, or yelling, please.
2. Students are still "in school." All school rules apply.
3. Students cannot bring electronic devices. These distract from the purpose of the field trip.
4. Students must stay with their assigned groups at all times except lunch. No visits to other groups under any circumstances. This rule is important so students complete the tasks assigned.
5. Students must pick up all litter they have left as well as the litter others may have left behind.
6. Plan a signal, such as a whistle, to which all students respond. This should be used to indicate a general gathering time.

Remember, all your students will not be perfect. Remain patient, keep a sense of humor, but if a student is in flagrant violation of the rules, be prepared to return him or her to school.

Field Trip:

Helpers

The success of a field trip depends on many things, not the least of which are the field trip helpers. As the size of the group expands, the number of helpers necessarily increases.

Teachers

If you are taking a single self-contained class, this planning is simple. One teacher, plus parent helpers, is adequate. Taking two teachers is preferable. Ask a music or art teacher to join you for the day.

The planning involved for a departmentalized middle school is more complex. Recruiting teachers from other departments is necessary if you plan to take an entire grade on the field trip. Having other teachers participate in this type of activity promotes total school involvement. When teachers from other departments are included, it is usually possible to get coverage for a class they may have on a different grade level by asking teachers who are "losing" a class for the day (i.e., one of the field trip classes) to cover for teachers who will be gone. Some school systems might arrange for substitutes.

Goodwill is important: Start planning early: If possible, give teachers a choice of sites. The music teacher may love the ocean; the language arts teacher may own the pond you are visiting.

You will need at least two meetings with these teachers to familiarize them with the ecology program goals, student activities, and the rules. (A sample letter to teachers detailing these instructions follows.)

Ideas for interdisciplinary activities will also evolve during these sessions. Participation of teachers from other departments gives them a vested interest in the extended activities of the science department.

Field Trip:

Sample Letter to Teachers

To: All Teachers on the Ecology Field Trip
From: Pat and Janet
Re: Here we go again for the "third time's a charm" Ecology Field Trip Day. We could never do this without all of you. Thank you for your help!!

To start things off:
You will be receiving today your packet and list of students and their individual groups (and list of aides, too—a few seventh graders and seven high school seniors are joining us this year. We expect to add parents, but do not have that list finalized yet). Please read your packet carefully. It is basically the same as last year with the addition of a weather forecasting section. Individual groups that have high school kids working with them will also have a minicourse taught to them sometime during the morning.

On Friday morning each site group (that is, OCEAN, FOREST, POND, MEADOW) will receive a brown paper bag full of the following:
1.   field guides for plants, animals, and insects (to be shared among all the groups on your sites)
2.   plastic bags
3.   extra packets for line transect work in case a student loses one or it falls into the stream or ocean
4.   one pair of binoculars to be shared
5.   extra meter sticks
6.   magnifying glasses
7.   an extra thermometer (be careful with it)
8.   a first aid kit

PLEASE BRING YOUR OWN WHISTLE (and extra pencils!!)

Goals

The kids will be working in the line transect groups this year that they have worked with for the past several weeks. Their basic goals are to survey and record all the living plants and animals within one meter of their 20-meter line (also anything that flies over the line counts), to decide on soil type, soil porosity, and to take several different kinds of temperature readings. In addition, they will sketch their community and spend at least 20 minutes as a large group in total (if possible) silence as they brainstorm to fill their language arts sheet with the sights, sounds, and smells of their community. They are to use field guides to help them identify plants and animals, and, if not successful, to describe the plant or animal carefully and in detail. They are also to make a legend to be used in placing their plants and animals on the line drawing.

If students should complete all the work in their packet, they should sit down and carefully fill out Activity 27 called "Analyzing a Community." This is an "extra" activity they normally would finish in the classroom.

Rules for the Day
- No destruction of property
- Work only with your specific group; no visits to other groups
- No electronic devices
- All school rules apply to this day

Weather
At the moment we do not have a rain date due to everyone's complicated schedule; therefore, we will go unless it is pouring or if it is just plain raining and the forecast is for that to continue all day. If gray or misty, we will still go. Students are being told to bring boots and rain gear. (Good idea for teachers, too.) They may come to school with their trip equipment and find the trip canceled. I hope teachers will be understanding. We don't have any lesson plans either. Hope for sun!!

Initial Schedule
Students will meet in the gym and gather in groups with their teachers according to their community assignments (OCEAN, FOREST, MEADOW, POND). Teachers will distribute the materials listed on page 1 of the student packet and discuss any last-minute problems. We plan to leave the gym about 8:45 a.m. after everyone has a last-minute bathroom run. Once on buses, you are on your own.

On Site
We suggest a quiet arrival and that you sit down together (put on the bug spray) and sketch your community. Last year at the end of the day at the pond, we added to the original sketch to see how much more students were noticing after a day spent at the pond.

Students may lay out line transects with your help; make sure there is variety of terrain covered, not just one long line of grass. It is good to have the line go over water at some point Students should put in at least two hours of good work on their plant and animal survey.

Lunch whenever it suits you.

Remind your high school students to teach their minicourse in the morning: Don't forget quiet time for the language arts activity, collecting of dead material (excluding teachers) at the end of the day for art collage making, and cleanup at the very end, of course. We have told students that this is not a course in the Destruction of Communities.

Return Schedule

By seventh period, we should all be back here at school. If it is a nice day, gather on the athletic field to turn in equipment and relax. We will now gather by divisions. All supplies and student packets are to be turned in to our room. Send a runner (the cleanest one) or an aide from each division to the science room with papers and tools. If the weather is bad, gather in the cafeteria. AND …

THANK YOU!

Field Trip:

Parents

Parents are crucial to the success and enthusiasm students will have for Field Trip Day. Include them whenever possible in the activities. A letter explaining Ecology Field Trip Day is important. Ask for those who wish to accompany the class. The ideal is to have one adult for every small group at a site. (If you have eight groups at the POND, you would do well with eight adults—two teachers and six parents.) Fathers and mothers enjoy the day. Do not encourage parents to bring small children.

Parents and nonscience teachers do not need environmental expertise. They may not know a white pine from a maple tree. The important requirement is interest and a willingness to be outside helping students explore.

Sample Letter to Parents

This letter is offered as an example of a way to include parents in your preparations and planning for a field trip. Their support and participation are important to the success of the field experience. Including background information about the trip makes the parents feel informed and positive about the trip.

Dear Parents,

We are embarking on another adventure in science—this time in the form of Ecology Field Trip Day. On Wednesday, May 23, sixth-grade students at BJHS will be traveling in groups of about 50 students with two teachers to four different community sites in the area—ocean, forest, field, and pond. We will be leaving the school about 8:45 a.m., spending the day at the site (eating a bag lunch), and returning to school by 1:15 p.m. While on site, students will be performing a variety of field tasks—surveying animal and plant populations, soil and temperature tests, language arts activities, art collecting, and mapping, all activities that we have been working on in school.

Language arts, science, social studies, art, music, and physical education teachers will accompany students in a truly interdisciplinary field day.

We need your cooperation in sending your child to school that day with boots, warm clothing, a sack lunch, and drink. Your child will have a checklist of "needs." In addition, we are eager to have parent volunteers accompany us on the field trip and spend the day outside working with young people. If interested, please sign the attached slip, return it with your child, and we will contact you. Thank you! We're hoping for a sunny day Wednesday.

Yes, I would like to volunteer to help with Ecology Field Trip Day. I would prefer to go to the _____.

Name _____ Telephone _____

Field Trip:

Peers

If your school has peer science helpers, have selected students accompany your classes on the field trip. In our program (see "High School and Peer Leadership" in Section I) seventh-grade students who were dedicated and competent proved to be extremely helpful and substituted for adults with some groups. It is important that the peers know the rules and understand they must work with their assigned group. This applies to high school students who also might accompany middle school students on the field trip.

In the case of high school students, they may also have a specific science lesson to teach to their small group. This is another way to make the day special.

Field Trip:

Grouping

Field trip groups may be organized in a variety of ways. Site selections will be the determiner of your class groupings.

1. If you are working with one self-contained classroom, you may select only two locations for the field trip and work with small groups in each half of the class. These groups can compare results and look for reasons for differences in results at the end of the day.

2. If you are working with one class, but are planning a cooperative field trip with other classes from your grade level, you may wish to mix the groups and follow the plan for four sites and several divisions of one grade level.

3. If you are working with one or many classes, once you have selected your field trip site, each class is assigned a group that corresponds to a location. For example, four sites might be POND, FOREST, OCEAN, MEADOW. In a class of 24, six students would become POND members, six OCEAN members, six FOREST members, six MEADOW members.

    These groups ideally should be formed at the beginning of the ecology unit. (See Activity 21.) They should work together for eight weeks on the activities in Section II. This greatly improves cooperation on field trip day. Leaders have evolved, groups have tried problem-solving processes, and you can assign tasks according to interests. An additional benefit is that you will have an opportunity to observe any potentially disastrous combinations of students, and you can rearrange the groups if necessary. (This particular grouping system provides the basis for the "Model for Departmentalized Trip With 200 Students," that follows.)

4. Assuming you are teaching several classes this way, each class will have the groups of OCEAN, FOREST, MEADOW, POND.

Field Trip:

Model for a Departmentalized Trip With 200 Students

- Eight sixth-grade classes are taking part in this field trip.
- Each class has 24 students.
- Each class has four field trip site groups (OCEAN, FOREST, MEADOW, POND) who have been working together for several weeks.
- On the day of the field trip each site group meets and travels on one bus—all OCEAN groups meet together and travel on one bus; all MEADOW groups meet and travel on another bus, and so on. Each site group is accompanied by the assigned teachers and parent volunteers.
- It is wise to have one parent drive, so there will be a vehicle on site in case of an emergency.
- Early in the morning of the field trip day, divide the gym or other large meeting area into four big sections (use masking tape on the floor). Have large signs designate each quarter as OCEAN, FOREST, POND, MEADOW and smaller signs indicate the location for each group from each class.

1 2 3 4 5 6 7 8 Meadow	1 2 3 4 5 6 7 8 Ocean
1 2 3 4 5 6 7 8 Pond	1 2 3 4 5 6 7 8 Forest

- A large brown paper bag containing the necessary materials marked for each group should sit at the head of each line. See Activity 36 for materials listings.
- All packets for each group should be stacked at the head of the line next to the paper bag.
- Each teacher in charge of a field trip site should also have a brown paper bag with extra materials and a few extra packets. (See "Sample Letter to Teachers" for a listing of these materials.) A few student packets (and once in a while a student) inevitably get wet. Material can be shared if they run short.
- A whistle comes in handy. Once all students are seated, go over any last-minute instruction changes, repeat the rules for field trips (See "Site Selection and Preliminary Arrangements"), and send students in small groups for the last-minute bathroom visit. Check to see if any students are missing lunches or their packets.
- Be sure teachers and parents are with their assigned groups.
- Have group leaders check their brown bags to make sure all supplies are there.

- Group leaders hand out packets to each student. From this point on, the student is responsible for his or her own packet.
- Answer any last-minute questions.
- Students and teachers board buses and travel to field trip locations. A quiet arrival, with all the students sitting together and surveying and sketching the community keeps the beginning controlled.
- The day is devoted to activities in the Field Trip Packet and may be scheduled according to Activity 37. See also the "Sample Letter to Teachers."
- Capitalize on the students' curiosity. The field trip is structured to ensure success, but be willing to investigate the "unplanned event" too.
- When students return, they should gather at the original departure point. Bags with equipment should be returned to the teacher in charge of the site. All student field trip packets must be gathered by groups and returned (peer helpers come in handy here) to the science classroom. They will be used for Activities 37 and 38 as well as for some of the activities in Section IV.

Field Trip:
Preparing the Field Trip Packet

Activities to be completed on Field Trip Day will vary according to the goals and objectives for your particular program. Included here is a sample list of activities that will fill an on-site four-hour day (including lunch). These activities were selected based on completion of this ecology unit.

Page # in the Packet	Activity
1	36. What You Will Need
2	37. What You Will Do
3	43. Art—Sketching
4	21. Line transect
5	Blank paper (for line transect drawing)
6	Blank paper (for legend)
7	24. Classifying Soil Samples
8	25. Determining Soil Porosity
9	26. Temperature Influences on a Community
10	27. Analyzing a Community
11	40. Language Arts—Descriptive Writing
12,13,14	Blank paper student can use for poetry, diagramming a food web, or extra notes

Note: When placing Activities 24, 25, and 26 in the Field Trip Packet, use only the graph portion of these activities; the analysis questions may be done at a later time if you wish. Students will already have completed these for the soil sampling done at school.

You may also wish to have the students complete Activity 44 (collage making). If so, include Student Worksheet 44 in your Field Trip Packet.

Activity 41 (poetry) may be completed on-site or at school.

Asking students to illustrate any of the cycles (in Activities 32, 33, and 34) for their site is an extension of the material they have studied and a direct application to their fieldwork.

ACTIVITY

Community Survey Instructions:
What You Will Need

Introduction

Spend one period with your students carefully covering the materials needed for the field trip. Thorough preparation and planning will make the trip a smoother event.

Objective

The student will arrive on field trip day with all the necessary materials.

Materials

- Pencil
- Paper
- Field trip packet (which will include student worksheet 36 on the top)
- Felt-tip markers

Teacher Instructions

1. With felt-tip marker in large print, students should print the name of their assigned community on the first line of student worksheet 36. If you are taking a large number of students, all pond packets might use green markers, all forest packets brown, all ocean packets blue, and all meadow packets red.
2. Students should also print their last name on the front of the packet in large letters with the markers.
3. Students will be listing the supplies they need to bring from home. This list is on student worksheet 36, and they should copy that on a separate sheet of paper. Emphasize the importance of boots: If you plan to go on the field trip in all kinds of weather, rain gear may be an additional item to suggest. Add any items you think are needed to your list.
4. Explain again that the leader of each working group at the site will be responsible for the bag containing meter sticks, line transect, and other items.
5. When the students have made a list of items they need from home, go on to page 2 (Activity 37) of the field trip packet.
6. When you have completed this work, collect all packets. They will be redistributed the morning of the field trip. This ensures that no student leaves the work at home.

Name _____ Date _____

Community Survey Instructions:
What You Will Need

Your Community _____

YOU  bring

At school, your GROUP  gets

Boots
Warm clothing
Clipboard
This field trip packet
Pencils
Bug spray
Collecting jar or bag
Trowel
Lunch
Drink
Backpack

Meter sticks
Line transect
Thermometer
Masking tape
Water jug
Plastic bottle
Field guides

Extras might include:
Camera
Binoculars
Sketching pad

ACTIVITY

Community Survey Instructions:

What You Will Do

Introduction

This activity sheet outlines the organization for Field Trip Day. The teachers, parents, and students will use this as a guide to accomplish the assigned tasks for the day. You should review this worksheet with your students on the second class period prior to Field Trip Day.

Objective

The student will understand the time and order of events for the Field Trip Day and will perform accordingly.

Teacher Instructions

1. *Note:* All of the details for this activity are discussed in the Model for Departmentalized Trip With 200 Students on p. 197.
2. The students should turn to page 2 of their field trip packets to find student worksheet 37.
3. Go over each step carefully, asking the questions, and clearing up any confusion students may have.
4. Students should complete the clock faces on the worksheet, filling in the correct time schedule for each activity and any blanks with the necessary information.
5. Because students should have done most of these activities, they should be familiar with the expectations. Briefly review each worksheet in the packet.
6. Introduce any new material that they must do on the field trip but have not seen before. For example, recording sensory detail (Activity 40), poetry (Activity 41), and art (Activities 43 through 45) may be activities you are asking them to complete. They will need instructions for these.
7. Students must give special attention to the final entry on student worksheet 37, "Return to school." You should introduce today a clear understanding of the procedure you will use for gathering in the correct location and returning packets and equipment to the science room. Then repeat the procedures before you depart on Field Trip Day.

Community Survey Instructions:

What You Will Do

1. Meet in _____ and sit with your community group.

2. Leave _____ and travel

   to _____ .

3. Arrive _____ and unload.

4. All sit together, meet as a group, discuss the site and possible working spots.

5. SKETCH YOUR COMMUNITY.

6. As a group, with your adults and peer helpers, decide on line transect positions.

   Go to the assigned spot for your group. You will work there most of the day.

7. Stretch out your LINE TRANSECT.

8. Begin by counting and mapping . . .

ANIMALS PLANTS

Be sure you have a legend.

9. Do SOIL TYPE and SOIL GRAPH . . . and . . .

10. TEMPERATURE and SOIL POROSITY.

11. Hey, Hey, it's time for LUNCH!

12. And then QUIET TIME. Work on the SENSORY DETAILS for Language Arts.

13. Finish LINE TRANSECT.

14. Collect for ART.

15. Return to school.

ACTIVITY

Organization of Presentations

Introduction
As a culmination of the field trip experience, a presentation of the information to the class may be organized. This project uses the creativity of the group to convey the information they have learned about their community.

Objective
The student will create and participate in a presentation depicting the highlights of the survey tasks performed on Field Trip Day.

Materials
- Student worksheet 38
- Pen or pencil

Teacher Instructions
1. Distribute student worksheet 38. Review with students note-taking skills.
2. Introduce the Presentation Guidelines (at the end of this activity). Emphasize that the final grade will be based on the criteria you will outline for them. Have students take notes using student worksheet 38.
3. Go over the guidelines. Cover each area carefully, and encourage student questions.
4. A suggested time-line for the presentation activities is included. You can reproduce it for student use if you want. The longer students have to prepare and practice, the better the presentations will become.
5. Student groups for this activity are the same groups that worked together on Field Trip Day.
6. Student leaders occasionally have problems with the behavior of a group member. You should intercede as needed.
7. Insist that each group practice its entire presentation at least once before the actual performance.
8. Set aside one area of the room where all presentations will take place. Allow 20 to 25 minutes for each group to present its information.
9. Assign the date for each group to perform. All presentations take place on the assigned date. A group member's absence does not cancel the show. Someone else must take over for him or her.

Suggested Time Line for Presentations
(Based on a 45-minute class period)

Monday:
1. Group leaders submit list of names of students in their groups to teacher.
2. Lists identify leader and assistant leader.
3. Group leaders list each student's topic beside each student's name.
4. Members of each group take notes on the topic assigned.

Tuesday:
1. Group leaders take attendance.
2. Check to see what group members have for information.
3. Students complete research on topic.

Wednesday:
1. Assistant leaders take attendance.
2. For the first 15 minutes, students discuss the theme for their presentation. Leaders report decisions to teacher.
3. Students finish research or begin work on visual aids.

Thursday:
1. Assistant leaders take attendance.
2. Students work on visual aids, costumes, or script.

Friday:
1. Assistant leaders take attendance.
2. Students must begin memorizing parts and practicing.
3. Complete visual aids and costumes.

Monday:
1. Assistant leaders take attendance.
2. Have first run-through of entire group.
3. Discuss presentation with group. Suggest improvements.

Tuesday (and other days to accommodate the groups presenting):
PERFORMANCE DAY

ACTIVITY

Presentation Guidelines

Students who take notes will pay closer attention to the requirements for presentations. Distribute student worksheet 38 to the class. Present the following material to them and allow ample opportunity for questions and clarification of tasks.

Students should be aware of the presentation goal: to illustrate and explain the workings of a community through a live performance. Therefore, presentations should include all the information collected on Field Trip Day plus other details that can be added from the research during the following two weeks.

Presentations

I. Organization
 A. You have already selected a leader for your group. Please select an assistant leader.
 B. Organize your group into sections that will cover each of the areas you collected information on: animals, plants, soils, temperatures, conditions, energy flow, interrelationships, and any special features of your community.
 C. You must have visual aids to use in your presentation. Suggestions include posters, models, diagrams, transparencies, and live specimens. These need to be large and colored.
 D. There may be no words on your visual aids, but you can number parts of a diagram if you wish.
 E. Your visual aid needs to be appropriate for your topic. If your topic is soils, for instance, your visual aid would not be pictures of birds.
 F. Your group must select a theme for the presentation by_____.
 (date)
 Will you do a TV show, an interview, a camping trip, a puppet show, a visit from outer space, or do you have another idea?
 G. You will need to have costumes and props that relate to your topic for the final presentation.

II. Presenting the Information
 A. Each member of the group must have a speaking part.
 B. The parts must be memorized. No cue cards.
 C. Your group must function as a group. Do not allow one person to stand in front of the audience, say his or her lines, and then stop participating.
 D. You must prepare a quiz (give it to the teacher to duplicate for you) that covers the material in your presentation. Your group will give the quiz to the class, then collect and grade the quiz.

III. Grades
 Your grade will be based on the following:
 A. Interest and originality
 B. Use of visual aids
 C. Amount and accuracy of information
 D. Members of the group participating
 E. Costumes

Name _____ Date _____

Organization of Presentations

I. Organization

    A. _____

    B. _____

    C. _____

    D. _____

    E. _____

    F. _____

    G. _____

II. Presenting the Information

    A. _____

    B. _____

    C. _____

    D. _____

III. Grades
    Your grade will be based on the following:

    A. _____

    B. _____

    C. _____

    D. _____

    E. _____

 ACTIVITY

Presentation Evaluation

Introduction
Productions of student presentations are based on the students' analyses of the community they visited on Field Trip Day. Their goal is to portray accurately the elements of that community to the audience through a concrete, visual production centered around a theme.

Optional Objective
The student will evaluate the work of his or her peers by observing the presentation and completing an evaluation form.

Teacher Instructions
1. Teacher and students should have a copy of "Evaluation of *(Community Name)*", which follows these instructions. All categories should be incorporated into the presentation.
2. The evaluation sheet is used as a checklist (objective).
3. The subjective aspect of the evaluation involves your own judgment of the creative aspect of each presentation.
4. Integrating all aspects of the presentation is difficult for most student groups. Suggestions when evaluating the groups after considering III. A through III. E on the Student Guidelines in Activity 38 could include considering if the group
   a. used creative ideas to carry out the theme?
   b. created costumes to support the theme?
   c. used many, detailed, and complete visual aids?
   d. worked together rather than have each student simply recite a part?
   e. went out of their way to collect all of the props that made the presentation seem realistic?
   f. went into great depth when covering certain aspects of the subject?
   g. located other information to enhance the subject?
   h. did anything unusual to keep the attention of the audience?
   i. incorporated all of the students in their group into the presentation? Did all of the students work to the best of their abilities?
5. At the conclusion of each presentation have the audience discuss three ideas:
   a. What did this group do particularly well as a part of this presentation?
   b. What might have improved this presentation?
   c. What was the most surprising piece of information you learned from this presentation?
6. Have each student submit an evaluation sheet for each group presentation (optional).

7. Each member of a group receives the same grade for the presentation unless there are unusual circumstances.

8. Presentations could be used as the culminating activity for a research project. If you are unable to participate in a field trip, students in groups can be assigned communities to research in the library and present to their classes.

ACTIVITY

EVALUATION of _____
(Community Name)

Title of Presentation _____

Yes/No	Comments
Theme	
Visual Aids	
Costumes	
Props	
All had parts	
Worked as a group	
Quiz	

Presentation covered

animals _____

plants _____

soils _____

temperatures _____

other conditions _____

interrelationships _____

special features _____

Any special comments?

Group members:

Grade:

SECTION IV
Integration and Extension

Overview

Activities in the field provide students with opportunities to be creative in the classroom. Integrating these experiences into the whole curriculum allows an interdisciplinary approach to education. Section IV, "Integration and Extension," provides some ideas with which to begin this process with your students. The areas addressed in this section are creative writing, art, social studies, and extended science activities. In addition, we encourage writing activities of all kinds in response to any of the activities you undertake.

A concern and understanding for the environment is an integral part of this program. Teachers are urged to repeat some of the initial activities to evaluate the growth students have made through this education in ecological principles. Activities 1, "At Issue," and 3, "A Sensory Approach to Ecology," can measure attitudinal changes that have occurred.

The future of this planet rests with the action of its inhabitants. The planet is one large ecosystem. By gaining knowledge and discussing observations, students also gain understanding. The better our future inhabitants understand the interrelationships on this planet, the greater hope we all have for survival.

Language Arts:
Using Sensory Details

Introduction

Employing the senses—smell, touch, hearing, and sight—will heighten the students' use of creative metaphor. The sensory details collected in the field can be transposed into enjoyable writing in the classroom.

Objective

The student will list sensory details and use them in developing poetry and essays or other writing activities reflecting the field trip environment.

Materials

- Student worksheet 40
- Pen or pencil
- Folder to write on

Teacher Instructions

1. Student worksheet 40 should be included in the Field Trip Packet (or use the activity alone during a 20-minute period outside the school building).
2. Sometime during the field experience (after lunch is a nice time), have students take out the worksheet and complete each list, filling in every blank. Otherwise, the students should work hard to experience their surroundings. The rule of silence is necessary to hear sounds and truly concentrate on the environment. Students may include details they have experienced during the day while working on their community survey tasks.
3. When you return to the classroom, these sheets should be removed from the packet and collected by the teacher. If your options are limited for interdisciplinary work, provide the time for this activity during science class.
4. If you have a self-contained class, you can use these sheets to construct paragraphs or poetry as your curriculum allows.

National Science Teachers Association

Using Sensory Details

Place _____

Below, list details about the environment that fall into these four sensory categories.

sight
sound
smell
touch

 ACTIVITY

Language Arts:
Writing an Acrostic Poem

Introduction
To integrate language experience into the field trip activity, capitalize on the name of the field trip community your students survey.

Objective
The student will write an acrostic poem based on his or her visit to a field trip site.

Materials
- Paper
- Pencil for each student

Teacher Instructions
1. Students should write the name of the community they are surveying vertically on their papers. The word (pond, field, ocean, lake, or forest) may appear in any location on the paper.
2. Using the letters in that word, students construct a poem expressing their feelings and ideas about the site they have visited. The lines of the poem do not need to rhyme. Rather, it is important that the poem reflects student's feelings about the field trip site.

Examples:

      Finding lots of
      Interesting
wEeds.
      Look! A
birD flies overhead.

      Flowers,
      lOgs,
      Robins
      Eating
wormS and
      naTure all around.

National Science Teachers Association

Social Studies:

*Mapping Your Local Community**

Before setting forth on a field trip, you can take advantage of the map skills your students have already learned in social studies.

Objective

The student will identify and survey a field trip site using a topographic map. The student will compare this specific site to a larger area.

Materials

- Student worksheet 42
- Pen or pencil
- Topographic survey maps of your field trip areas
- Local map
- World atlas
- World maps

Teacher Instructions

1. Introduce this activity by discussing the proposed science field trip. Ask students to identify the site their group will be visiting and surveying (for example, a field on Old Farm Road or a riverbank along River Drive). Students should work together in their field trip site groups for this activity.
2. Have students consider these questions: How can we locate field trip sites before we arrive? Can we learn anything about the area without seeing it? What would you use to do that? (Maps and atlases or gazetteers.)
3. Distribute student worksheet 42, topographic survey maps, and atlas to the class.
4. Students should follow the directions on the worksheets and complete the data.
5. You should supervise the groups as they work. As they complete the local information, each group should then use a world atlas to form a bigger and better picture of the site in relation to the United States. Thoroughly discuss the results from each group when the work is completed.
6. After students return from the field trip, compare the answers on these worksheets with the data students gathered on site.
7. A discussion of how an atlas could be put together might be appropriate. An extension of this activity might be to construct a local atlas based on the information students can provide with research skills.

Question 15 on student worksheet 42: Physiography is physical geography.

*Activity adapted by permission of John E. Paige, Brunswick, ME.

Name _____ Date _____

Mapping Your Local Community

Part I. Locating the Field Trip Site

1. Locate your field trip site. Write directions that the school bus will follow to arrive at your field trip spot.

    _____

    _____

    _____

    _____

2. What is the classification of the road leading to the site? _____

    _____

3. If you followed the road, what town would you reach?

    _____

4. How many miles is it from school to the site? _____

5. What is the approximate elevation of the site? _____

6. What symbol represents your school? _____

7. What county are you in? _____

8. On the map you will see wavy lines called contour lines. What do these lines indicate?

    _____

    If they are close together, what does that tell you?

    _____

Name _____ Date _____ ㊷

Part II. Town and State

9. Use the index in the back of an atlas. Locate your town and record the exact latitude and longitude.

   _____

10. Turn to the page listed for your town, and locate it. What city lies due east of

    your town? _____ northwest? _____

11. Locate the section titled land forms. Name two land forms in your state.

    _____

12. Find the page on annual rainfall. How many centimeters (or inches) of rainfall

    occur in your area each year?

    _____

13. In the index, find a page that will tell you about vegetation. Read that page, and record the type of vegetation found in your state. Explain what these words mean. Use a dictionary if you need one. Mention specific trees.

    _____

    _____

    _____

    _____

14. What environment is listed for your area?

    _____

    _____

15. Define physiography in your own words.

    _____

    _____

Name _____ Date _____

What kind of physiography is found in your state?

_____

_____

_____

Part III. World Regions

16. On what continent is your town located? _____

17. In which two hemispheres is your town located?

    _____

18. In what latitude zone is your town? _____

19. In what country is your state? _____

20. Is your town near an ocean or large lake?_____

    Name it. _____

21. In which direction do prevailing winds blow?

    _____

22. What climate type is found in your state?

    _____

23. Write a description of this climate.

    _____

    _____

    _____

24. Where else in the world might this climate be found?

    _____

    _____

    _____

Art:

Sketching a Community

Introduction

The benefit of this activity is that it will allow students to concentrate on observing the parts of the community as scenes of beauty. They should be using this actual field trip experience to draw what they see, not just what they might imagine.

Objective

The student will observe his or her surroundings and sketch the community.

Materials

- Student worksheet 43
- Pencil
- Colored pencils if students wish

Teacher Instructions

1. As students arrive at a community site, find a place where they can sit and quietly observe the entire site without moving around. For example, there might be a slight rise near the edge of a pond. Gather the group at that spot for this activity.
2. Identify for them and then have them sketch in the boundaries of the community.
3. Students should spend 15 minutes sketching all parts of the community.
4. At the end of the field trip, students should return to this original sketch location and take out the drawings they did upon arrival. Now they should add any other things they did not observe originally. The emphasis is on a complete drawing.
5. Students may take these original sketches and make a finished watercolor, crayon, or pen and ink drawing of their community when they return to class.

Sketching a Community

Find a spot where you can see the whole community that you will be studying today. Your teacher will identify the boundaries for you. Sketch all of the things that you can see. At the end of the day and your work at this site, you will return to your "sketching" spot and add any things you did not notice when you first arrived. You may wish to use this sketch as the basis for a finished art piece (watercolor, pen and ink, or crayon) when you return to school.

Art:
Making a Collage

Introduction

This art project can be a part of the Field Trip Packet. You could also organize a separate collecting trip. The items collected can be stored until your class has time to work on the project. If you are in a departmentalized program, the art teacher may be willing to coordinate this project for your students.

Objective

The student will collect objects during the field trip to construct a collage.

Materials

For gathering:
- Large plastic ziplock bags, one per student
- Masking tape
- Felt-tip pens
- Large brown grocery bags
- Student worksheet 44

For pressing:
- Newspapers
- Large, heavy books

For making collages:
- Large manila drawing paper
- White glue
- Collected items
- Felt-tip pens

Teacher Instructions

1. Students should write their names on masking tape and then put the tape on plastic bags for future identification.
2. Distribute student worksheet 44, or make sure it is included in the Field Trip Packet (see Section III).
3. Discuss the idea of a collage, how collages are arranged, and the themes inherent in most collages. Perhaps you will have some examples to show or students will have made collages for other classes.

4. Read and discuss with students the items on the "Suggested Collectibles" list. At the same time, go over health and safety concerns.
5. Brainstorm with students for ideas of other items that could also appear on the collecting list. Live animals are not a possibility! Live plants, such as leaves, ferns or flowers, may be gathered with the following precautions: Samples should be small and easy to press, and samples must not be of endangered species.
6. After completing the trip and any necessary pressing, collect individual student bags and store them in the large brown bags. You can distribute the bags when the class is ready to work on the collages.

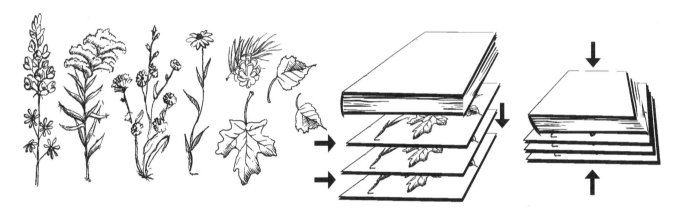

Making the Collages

1. Review the concept of collage.
2. Distribute drawing paper that will be the background for the collage.
3. Students should empty their collections and spread the contents out on their desks.
4. Some students will compose pictures or scenes, while others may choose to arrange patterns or designs.
5. Once the final collage is arranged, students can glue collected items onto the background.
6. Students may want to fill in bare spots with line drawings or may choose to trade items with other students to expand the individual's collage.
7. Composing titles for the artworks provides another creative aspect to this project.

Making a Collage

The items on this list are suggestions of things you will collect to use for an art project. Remember that you will be creating a picture from these items, so here are a few hints to keep in mind:

- Objects should be small.
- Do not destroy other living things in the search. Choose items that are already on the ground.
- Pick only a few wildflowers or leaves or ferns. Press any leaf-type plant immediately.
- Keep all items in your ziplock bags. Make sure your name is on your bag.

Suggested collectibles
- Dry grasses
- Leaves—assorted sizes and shapes
- Nuts, acorns, pine cones, spruce cones
- Acceptable wild flowers (press them)
- Small colorful stones
- Shells
- Seaweed (preferably dry)
- Unusual small pieces of wood
- Bird feathers
- Ferns (press)
- Mosses (press)

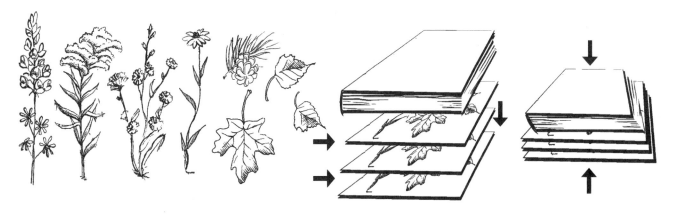

 ACTIVITY

Art:
What Colors Can You Find in a Meadow?

Introduction
This art activity is designed to encourage students to look at a community from a new perspective. Most of the students' previous tasks have focused on process skills requiring analysis, identification, classification, or experimentation. Now they will be going into a meadow, or other site, with eyes attuned to color and beauty. Since this activity involves "picked" items, plan and use it cautiously. As always, emphasize health and safety.

Objective
The student will be able to locate and identify several shades of one color (or a rainbow spectrum) within a particular environment.

Materials
- White paper for each student
- Glue

Teacher Instructions
1. When students arrive at a particular environmental site (either on the field trip or as a homework assignment), ask them to look carefully at the colors displayed.
2. Challenge the students to find 10 varying shades of one particular color, or the seven colors of the rainbow: red, orange, yellow, green, blue, indigo, violet.
3. Students may go into the meadow and gather a tiny piece of each color, if the item is plentiful.
4. Items such as leaves or wildflowers will need to be pressed. (See Activity 44.)
5. Students should glue their colors on the white paper. Label accordingly, if desired.

Science:

The Parts of the Biosphere

From the NSES—p. 158

The idea of systems provides a framework in which students can investigate the four major interacting components of the earth system—geosphere (crust, mantle, and core), hydrosphere (water), atmosphere (air), and the biosphere (the realm of all living things).

Objective

The student will identify the parts of the biosphere and the composition of its major biomes.

SCILINKS®
THE WORLD'S A CLICK AWAY

Topic: populations,
   communities,
   ecosystems
Go to: *www.scilinks.org*
Code: EXPL17

Materials

- Biosphere puzzle (one per student or group)
- Student worksheet 46
- Pen or pencil
- Scissors
- Colored pencils
- White glue
- Stiff paper
- Reference books

Teacher Instructions

1. Duplicate enough copies of the three puzzle pages that follow for each member or each group in the class.
2. Distribute the puzzles to individual students or groups.
3. Students work together to cut out the puzzles and put them together.
4. Using the visual information within the puzzles, students should complete the first three columns of Data Chart 46. The remainder of the information can be obtained by using reference books or the internet.
5. You should circulate throughout the class during this activity and help when needed.
6. At the conclusion of the activity, you should conduct a major class discussion covering the information that students are gathering in this and other activities. The following are suggested questions that might instigate thoughtful conversation:
   a. Define biosphere (the environment in which one lives, acts, or has influence; the Earth); biome (a region of similar vegetation governed by climate covering a large area and containing a large community of plants and animals); ecosystem (combination of a habitat with a plant and animal community).

ACTIVITY

46

b. Compare larger and smaller areas. What do all of these have in common? (Water, land, and air.) What characteristics are different? (The populations that live there.)

c. Which of these factors, water, land, or air, has the greatest influence on the climate of the biome? (Water, in the form of varying rainfall.)

d. How does the climate affect living things? (It creates the conditions for living things to exist.)

e. Is it possible to cause a biome to change? (Yes.) Who might cause such a change? (People.) How? (They create changes in the Earth's surface or population changes.)

f. Is it possible to change the parts of the biosphere? (Yes.) Who might cause such a change? (People.) How? (They emit pollutants into the environment.)

g. Will changing any one of these affect the entire planet? (Yes.) Which one might do this and why? (Pollutants that affect climatic changes could affect the entire planet: the greenhouse effect.)

7. Students could locate current articles in newspapers and magazines and use these to substantiate and support particular points of view in these discussions.

8. Use your bulletin board to display these articles and continue the conversations.

9. Capitalize on the students' enthusiasm by having them write to elected officials or write letters to the editor of the local newspaper. Perhaps the school newspaper would be interested in covering your class's activities. Students may wish to write to national magazines expressing concern for the need to support an ecologic approach to life on Earth.

The Parts of the Biosphere

1. Take the puzzle you have received, cut out the pieces, and put the pieces together. Glue them on the stiff paper.
2. When you have correctly finished the work, observe the pictures carefully. Fill in the first three columns of the data chart below. Complete the rest of the information on the chart by using reference books.

Data Chart 46

biome name	unique characteristics	organisms	rainfall	location

3. Answer these questions:
   a. Define these terms:

   planet Earth_____

   biosphere _____

   biome _____

b . List the four characteristics that these areas have in common.

_____

_____

_____

_____

c. Which of these four factors has the greatest influence on the climate of the biome?

_____

d. How does climate affect living things? _____

_____

e. What factor would be most likely to cause a major change in a biome? Why?

_____

_____

f. Could that factor be strong enough to cause a change in the entire planet? Why or why not? _____

_____

_____

_____

g. Support your answer with an article from the newspaper or a recent magazine.

_____

_____

_____

_____

_____

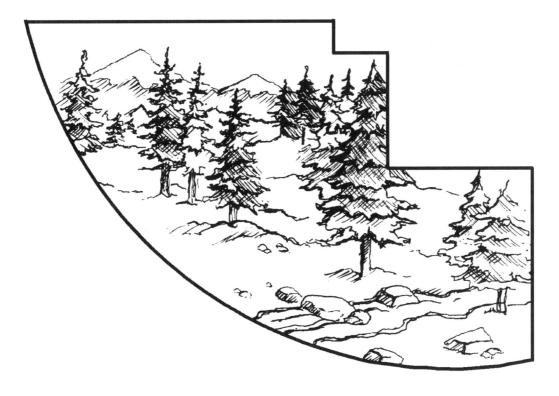

Name _____ Date _____

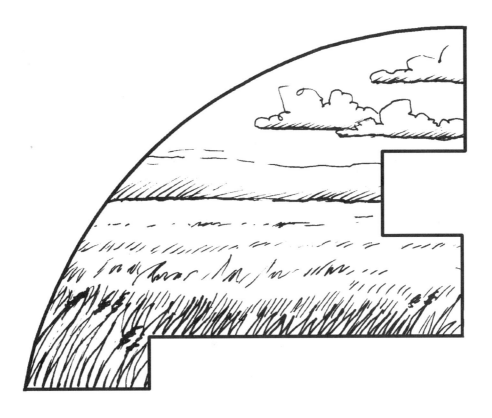

ACTIVITY

Science:
Build Your Own Ecosystem

Topic: populations, communities, ecosystems
Go to: *www.scilinks.org*
Code: EXPL17

Introduction
You can encourage daily observation of the relationships among living things by creating a terrarium, a simple but messy activity. This plan is for a woodland terrarium. With minor adaptations, you can create any type of habitat.

From the NSES—p. 141
Although men and women using scientific inquiry have learned much about object, events, and phenomena in nature, much more remains to be understood. Science will never be finished.

Objective
The student will build a terrarium and observe relationships of living things in their environment.

Materials
- Student worksheet 47
- Clear, clean containers (1-liter soft-drink containers and gallon jars work well)
- Soil
- Charcoal and gravel (available at greenhouses or pet shops)
- Newspapers
- Collecting bags
- Margarine tubs for insects and animals
- Sticks or spoons for planting
- Modeling clay to keep containers from rolling

Teacher Instructions
1. Review the meaning of ecosystem (plants and animals living in the same habitat). Discuss the concept of survival based on the relationships within the habitat. Explain that the making of an ecosystem will allow students to observe the relationships closely.
2. Follow the instructions on student worksheet 47 for "Preparing the Container."
3. The site for collection may be close by, or you may wish to travel to an area farther away. See details of field trip in Section III. Be sure to review safety information.
4. Woodland terraria can be very successful. Go over the suggestions on student worksheet 47 with your students.
5. Follow the instructions on student worksheet 47 for "Planting the Terrarium." *Note:* This activity could be done as a home project rather than an in-class activity.

National Science Teachers Association

Build Your Own Ecosystem

The construction of your own ecosystem will allow you to observe the life cycles of the living things in that system. This plan is for a woodland terrarium, but you could build a desert ecosystem or aquatic ecosystem as well.

Preparing the Container

1. Spread newspapers on your desk.

2. Decide on the final position in which your container will rest. If your container is round, you can use clay to keep it from rolling.

3. Put a 1-inch layer of charcoal and aquarium stones in the container. Spread it out evenly.

4. Cover this layer with a 2- to 4-inch layer of soil. Use regular soil or potting soil mixed with regular soil. Add water to moisten soil thoroughly.

5. Smooth the soil evenly.

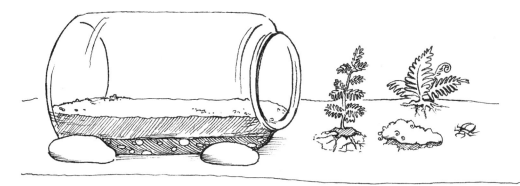

Collecting the Living Things

1. Collect only enough plants to fill the container. You do not want it too crowded.

2. Species of mosses and small ferns make a good base. Small wildflowers or plants with berries will be pretty. You might find a tiny tree.

3. Dig around the roots of the flowers and trees. Because mosses and ferns do not have true roots, take the soil with them to make sure they will grow.

Name _____ Date _____

4. Look for interesting rocks, lichens, and unusual seeds to add to your habitat.

5. You may find an insect, newt, salamander, snake, or toad that would enjoy your terrarium. If you collect animals, you must provide food. You should put them back in the wild within two weeks.

Planting the Terrarium

1. Arrange your plants in the container until they please you.

2. Plant the flowers and trees. Push moss and ferns into the soil with your hands.

3. Add the rocks, sticks, lichens, and seeds.

4. Put any animals in last.

5. Put a piece of clear plastic wrap tightly across the opening of the container. A rubber band or tape will hold it in place.

6. Put your terrarium in a spot where there is light, but not direct sun.

Caring for the Terrarium

1. Check for water. If there are water drops on the plastic wrap your terrarium is fine. If not, sprinkle (do not pour) with water.

2. Feed animals. Look in science and nature books to find the proper food suggestions.

3. Observe and record information on some of the life cycles you have studied in ecology. Ask yourself, where does my animal get oxygen? Where did those drops of water on the plastic wrap come from? How is this terrarium like my planet?

National Science Teachers Association

Science:

How Pollutants Affect a Yeast Culture

Introduction

For a community to maintain a quality of life, it must control pollutants. Pollutants can be harmful to living things in an ecosystem. In this experiment, students will observe and record the results of pollution in a yeast colony.

Topic: pollutions,
Go to: *www.scilinks.org*
Code: EXPL237

From the NSES—p. 140

Pollution is a change in the environment that can influence the health, survival, or activities of organisms, including humans.

Objective

The student will experiment with pollution in a yeast colony and make inferences based on the results as to the effect of polluting substances on living things.

Materials

- Yeast
- Bromthymol blue pH indicator (available at aquarium supply stores)
- Test tubes (4 per group)
- Test-tube rack
- Marker
- Saltwater
- Liquid soap
- Eye droppers

Teacher Instructions

1. Yeast may be purchased in any grocery store. To prepare the living yeast colony, mix 1 envelope of yeast with 1/2 cup very warm water.
2. The nonliving colony can be made by using cold water rather than warm.
3. Prepare salt water by adding 2 grams of salt (NaCl) to 100 ml of water.
4. Distribute student worksheet 48.
5. Organize and perform the experiment according to the instructions on the student worksheet.
6. Experiments should be stored in a safe place for about 24 hours.
7. In class the following day, students should make observations and record the data on their data tables.

8. After recording the data, students should answer the questions on the activity sheet.

9. At the conclusion of this experiment, you should discuss the results with your students. Extend the discussion to relate to the environment. Questions for discussion might include:

   a. What actual living things in the environment would yeast represent? (The decomposers.)

   b. Is there any real possibility that salt or soap is dumped into the environment? (Salt from roads and soap waste from homes and industry.)

   c. What danger occurs to the environment if decomposers are killed by pollutants? (The rate and efficiency of decomposition is impaired, causing a reduction in necessary nutrients and gases being returned to the soil. Soils become barren, plant growth is reduced, and the oxygen supply is reduced. Ultimately, the entire biosphere (all of the planet Earth) is endangered.

Teacher Information:

Yeast will form a living colony under the proper conditions. Warm water will activate the yeast colony. Bromthymol blue is a pH indicator. It changes color in the presence of acids and bases. Living yeast colonies release carbon dioxide gas during respiration. CO_2 has a tendency to be slightly basic rather than acidic. If the solution in the test tube changes from blue to green, the indication is that the life processes are not interrupted. The solution color progresses from blue to green to yellow to red, as the pollutants cause the culture conditions to change from a basic to an acidic condition where life processes would be interrupted and the yeast would die.

How Pollutants Affect a Yeast Culture

Pollutants can be harmful to the living things in an ecosystem. This experiment will show you how simple substances can affect a yeast colony.

Part I. Setting up the Experiment

A. Your group needs these materials: 4 test tubes, test-tube rack, marker, liquid soap, saltwater, living yeast culture, nonliving yeast culture, eye dropper.

B. Label your test tubes #1, #2, #3, and #4 with the marker. Place them in the test-tube rack.

C. Organize the experiment as follows:

Test tube #1: 10 drops of the living yeast culture

Test tube #2: 10 drops saltwater plus 10 drops living yeast culture

Test tube #3: 10 drops liquid soap plus 10 drops living yeast culture

Test tube #4: 10 drops nonliving yeast culture

D. Add 10 drops of bromthymol blue pH indicator to each test tube.

Part II. Recording Data

A. Record the following information for Day 1:

Data Table 48: What Color Is the Liquid in Each Test Tube?

test tube	date	color	date	color
#1 living yeast				
#2 living yeast + saltwater				
#3 living yeast + soap				
#4 nonliving yeast				

B. Put rack in a safe place for 24 hours.

C. After the 24 hours are up, retrieve your experiment and observe each test tube.

1. Record any color changes for the second day. *Note:* Blue liquid changes to green if carbon dioxide gas is present.

Name _____ Date _____

2. Clean out your experiment by dumping it into the sink. Wash test tubes with soap and water, and put the materials away.

Part III. Results and Conclusions

A. Consult your data table. Explain why the bromthymol blue indicator changed color. _____

_____

B. Where did the carbon dioxide gas come from? _____

_____

_____

C. Did the pollutants in test tubes #2 and #3 affect the living cultures? How do you know? _____

_____

_____

_____

D. What is the reason for setting up test tubes #1 and #4? _____

_____

_____

E. Do you know of any situation when either salt or soap might be released into the environment? _____

_____

_____

F. Explain what part small living things like yeast colonies play in the environment.

_____

_____

G. If pollutants can kill this part of the food web, how might that affect the entire environment? _____

_____

_____

H. List ways that pollutants can be controlled to prevent their negative effect on the environment. _____

_____

_____

Science:
A Plant Scavenger Hunt

Objective

The student will compete at collecting and identifying common plants. The plants used in this activity are common on the East Coast, down through Virginia and possibly Georgia. If they don't exist in your area, you can write clues based on common local plants.

Materials

- Student worksheet 49
- Pencil
- Field guides
- Prizes for winners

Teacher Instructions

1. Students should look at student worksheet 49, read each clue silently, and write the name of the correct plant next to the same number at the bottom of the worksheet (Allow 5 to 10 minutes for this.)
2. You may allow the students to work in small groups to determine answers. This part of the activity is less important than the following outside work.
3. At the conclusion of the allotted time, read each clue and give the correct name of each plant.
4. Students will go outside to hunt for the plants. The students with all the correct identifications in the field are the winners of the scavenger hunt.
5. The teacher is not a resource for this activity. You may give no answers.
6. The field guides should provide the resources students need for proper identification.
7. The clues on the worksheet were written for the Northeast. You can adapt clues to fit your own area.
8. Award prizes to students. Ties will occur if you allow the winners to be those who have most correct rather than all correct.

Answers to student worksheet 49

1. British soldiers
2. Oak
3. Broom moss
4. Maple
5. Cranberry

6. Goldenrod
7. White pine
8. Cinnamon
9. Peat moss (sphagnum)
10. Birch

Name _____ Date _____

A Plant Scavenger Hunt

1. Read each of the following clues on the worksheet. Identify the plant, and write its name beside the correct number at the bottom of the page.

2. If you cannot identify the plant, skip that clue and go on to the next one. Your teacher will review the correct answers with the class.

Plant Scavenger Hunt Clues

1. These lichens you might have found during the American Revolutionary War.

2. Plant an acorn, and you will have a tree. Find a leaf from this kind of tree.

3. You could use this type of moss to sweep the floor.

4. Find a leaf from the tree that has the same name as the syrup for your pancakes.

5. The Pilgrims may have used this plant at their Thanksgiving feast.

6. The name of this plant is the color of a high-priced metal and ends with a type of stick.

7. The name of this tree starts with the color of snow and ends with a rhyme for the word *sign*.

8. This fern is named for a spice you might sprinkle on your toast.

9. In some countries, this moss is burned for fuel.

10. Native Americans used the bark of this tree to build their canoes.

Your answers:

1. _____   2. _____

3. _____   4. _____

5. _____   6. _____

7. _____   8. _____

9. _____   10. _____

National Science Teachers Association

Bibliography

Allaby, M. 1999. *Biomes of the world*. Danbury, CT: Grolier Educational.

Allaby, M., and I. Crofton. 2002. *Deserts and semi-deserts*. Austin, TX: Raintree/Steck-Vaughn.

Anderson, M. K. 1990. *Oil spills*. New York: Franklin Watts.

Andrews and McMeel. 1990. *Earth works: 50 simple things kids can do to save the Earth*. Kansas City, MO: Andrews and McMeel.

Ausubel, David P. 1967. *Learning theory and classroom practice*. Ontario: The Ontario Institute for Studies in Education.

Banks, M. 1988. *Endangered wildlife*. Vero Beach, FL: Rourke Enterprises.

Beatty, R. 2003. *Wetlands*. Austin, TX: Raintree/Steck-Vaughn.

Bocknek, J. 2003. *World fishing*. Mankato, MN: Smart Apple Media.

Buck, M. W. 1950. *In woods and fields*. New York: Abingdon Press.

Buck, M. W. 1952. *In yards and gardens*. New York: Abingdon-Cokesbury Press.

Buck, M. W. 1958. *Pets from the pond*. New York: Abingdon Press.

Burnie, D. 1994. *Dictionary of nature*. First American ed. London: Dorling Kindersley.

Burnie, D. 1994. *Life*. First American ed. London: Dorling Kindersley.

Caduto, M. J. 1985. *Pond and brook: A guide to nature in freshwater environments*. Hanover, NH: University Press of New England.

Cerullo, M. M., and J. L. Rotman. 1994. *Lobsters: Gangsters of the sea*. First ed. New York: Cobblehill Books.

Chinery, M. 2000. *Plants and planteaters*. New York: Crabtree.

Cochrane, J. 1987. *Urban ecology*. New York: Bookwright Press.

Cochrane, J., and C. Fitzsimons. 1988. *Land ecology*. New York: Bookwright Press.

Coulombe, D. A. 1984. *The seaside naturalist: A guide to nature study at the seashore*. Englewood Cliffs, NJ: Prentice-Hall.

De Luca, D. 2002. *Animal atlas*. Florence, Italy: McRae Books.

Dorling Kindersley. 1992. *Eyewitness visual dictionary of plants*. First American ed. New York: Dorling Kindersley.

Durrell, G. M., and L. Durrell. 1983, 1982. *The amateur naturalist*. New York: Knopf.

Evans, I. 1984. *Biology: Plants, animals, and ecology*. New York: F. Watts.

Foran, J. 2003. *A planet choking on waste*. Mankato, MN: Smart Apple Media.

Goodnough, D. 2001. *Endangered animals of North America: A hot issue*. Berkeley Heights, NJ: Enslow.

Grant, L. 1993. *Great careers for people concerned about the environment*. U.S. ed. Detroit, MI: UXL.

Green, K. P. 2002. *Global warming: Understanding the debate*. Berkeley Heights, NJ: Enslow.

Grolier. 2000. *Plants and plant life*. 10 vols. Danbury, CT: Grolier .

Grolier Educational. 2000. *Under the microscope: Around people*. Danbury, CT: Grolier Educational.

Grolier Educational. 2000. *Under the microscope: Behavior*. Danbury, CT: Grolier Educational.

Grolier Educational. 2000. *Under the microscope: Habits*. Danbury, CT: Grolier Educational.

Grolier Educational. 2000. *Under the microscope: Homes*. Danbury, CT: Grolier Educational.

Grolier Educational. 2000. *Under the microscope: Lifecycles*. Danbury, CT: Grolier Educational.

Grolier Educational. 2000. *Under the microscope: On the move*. Danbury, CT: Grolier Educational.

Grolier Educational. 2000. *Under the microscope: Record-breakers*. Danbury, CT: Grolier Educational.

Hare, T. 1991. *Habitat destruction*. London: Gloucester Press.

Hayhurst, C. 2003. *Biofuel power of the future: New ways of turning organic matter into energy*. New York: Rosen Publishing Group.

Jennings, T. 2002. *Ecology: the study of living things*. Milwaukee, WI: Gareth Stevens.

Kallen, S. A. 2003. *Life on an ocean shore*. Farmington Hills, MI: KidHaven Press/Thomson/Gale.

Kowalski, K. M. 2004. *Global warming*. New York: Benchmark.

Lampton, C. 1998. *Endangered species*. New York: F. Watts.

Lilly, K., and B. Taylor. 1992. *The animal atlas*. 1st American ed. New York: Knopf.

Llewellyn, C. 2001. *Animal atlas*. Chicago: World Book.

Markham, A. 1988. *The environment*. Vero Beach, FL: Rourke Enterprises.

Markle, S. 1991. *The kids' earth handbook*. First ed. New York: Atheneum.

Marshall Cavendish. 2001. *Aquatic life of the world*. 11 vols. Tarrytown, NY: Marshall Cavendish.

Marshall Cavendish. 2000. *Exploring life science*. New York: Marshall Cavendish.

McCuen, M. 1999. *The world environment and the global economy*. Hudson, WI: GEM.

Mitchell, J. H. 1980. *The curious naturalist*. Englewood Cliffs, NJ: Prentice-Hall.

Nardo, D. 1990. *Oil spills*. San Diego, CA: Lucent Books.

National Research Council. 1996. *National Science Education Standards*. Washington, DC: National Academy Press. Available online at *www.nap.edu/books/0309053269/html/index.html*

Palmer, J. 1990. *Recycling metal*. New York: Franklin Watts.

Palmer, J. 1990. *Recycling plastic*. New York: Franklin Watts.

Parker, S. 2001. *Adaptation*. Chicago: Heinemann Library.

Parker, S. 2001. *Survival and change*. Chicago: Heinemann Library.

Parker, S., and P. Dowell. 1988. *Pond and river*. New York: Knopf.

Patent, D. H., and W. Munoz. 2003. *Life in a grassland*. Minneapolis, MN: Lerner.

Penny, M. 1991. *Protecting wildlife*. Austin, TX: Steck-Vaughn Library.

Pollock, S. 1993. *Ecology*. 1st American ed. London: Dorling Kindersley.

Pollock, S. 2000. *Ecology*. New York: Dorling Kindersley.

Rinard, J. E. 1987. *Wildlife making a comeback: How humans are helping*. Washington, DC: National Geographic Society.

Roberts, R. 1999. *Endangered species*. San Diego: Lucent.

Scoones, S. 2002. *Climate change: Our impact on the planet*. Austin, TX: Raintree/Steck-Vaughn.

Silverstein, A., and R. A. Silverstein. *Plants*. 1996. 1st ed. New York: Twenty-First Century Books.

Smith, T. 2003. *Earth's changing climate*. Mankato, MN: Smart Apple Media.

Snedden, R. 2003. *Plants and fungi: Multicelled life*. Chicago, IL: Heinemann Library.

Time Life. 1999. *Our environment*. Alexandria, VA: Time Life.

Waites, G. 1998. *The Cassell dictionary of biology*. London: Cassell.

Waldbauer, G. 1998. *The handy bug answer book*. Canton, MI: Visible Ink Press.

Walker, S. M. 2003. *Life in an estuary*. Minneapolis, MN: Lerner.

Wallace, H. 2001. *Food chains and webs*. Chicago: Heinemann Library.

Wallace, M. D. 1999. *America's mountains: A guide to plants and animals.*Golden, CO: Fulcrum.

Ward, C. 2002. *International wildlife encyclopedia*. Third ed. New York: Marshall Cavendish.

Weitz, M. 1992. *Poisoning the land*. New York: Gloucester Press.

Whitfield, P. 1989. *Can the whales be saved: Questions about the natural world and the threats to its survival*. New York: Kestrel.

Wong, O. K. *Hands-on ecology*. Chicago: Children's Press.

Woodward, J. 2002. *Temperate forests*. Austin, TX: Raintree/Steck-Vaughn.

Field Guides

Behler, J., and F. W. King. 2000. *The Audubon Society field guide to North American reptiles and amphibians*. New York: Alfred A. Knopf.

Burt, W., and R. Grossenheider. 1998. *A field guide to mammals* (Peterson Field Guide). Boston: Houghton Mifflin Company.

Foster, S., and R. A. Caras. 1994. *A field guide to venomous animals and poisonous plants, North America, north of Mexico*. Boston: Houghton Mifflin.

Meinkoth, N. A. 1981. *The Audubon Society field guide to North American seashore creatures*. New York: Knopf.

Mitchell, R., and H. Zim. 1977. Butterflies and moths. New York: Golden Press.

Peterson, R. T., and M. McKenny. 1998. *A field guide to wildflowers* (Peterson Field Guide). Boston: Houghton Mifflin Company.

Peterson, R. T., and G. Petrides. 1973. *A field guide to trees and shrubs* (Peterson Field Guide). Boston: Houghton Mifflin Company.

Reid, G. K. 1987. *A guide to common plants and animals of North American ponds and lakes*. New York: Golden Press.

Robbins, C., B. Bruun, and H. Zim. 1990. *A guide to field identification of birds of North America*. New York: Golden Press.

Shuttleworth, F., and H. Zim. 1987. *Mushrooms and other nonflowering plants*. New York: Golden Press.

Whitaker, J. O. 1996. *The Audubon Society field guide to North American mammals*. New York: Knopf.

Video, DVD, and Websites

Scientific method. 2002. Scottsdale, Arizona: Teacher's Video.

Pond and river. 1997. DK Vision.

The private life of plants. 1995. Atlanta: Turner Home Entertainment.

www.calacademy.org/exhibits/anwr
Arctic National Wildlife

ICYouSee: T is for thinking
www.ithaca.edu/library/Training/think.html
John Henderson is a reference librarian at the Ithaca College Library. He has been involved with the World Wide Web since 1994. This tutorial uses actual sites to illustrate its lessons. Users view multiple sites that provide different answers to the same question, helping reinforce an understanding of the need for references and credibility.

Resource Discovery Network
www.rdn.ac.uk
A consortium of more than 70 libraries and educational institutions developed the Resource Discovery Network. It serves as a hub that provides access to numerous subject directories. Note that the *Virtual Training Suite* allows users to select from a wide range of subject-based tutorials that focus on finding and using high quality Internet resources.

Maine Resources

Cerullo, M. M., and B. Curtsinger. 2003. *Life under ice*. Gardiner, ME: Tilbury House.
Cerullo, M. M., and B. Curtsinger. 1999. *Sea soup: Phytoplankton*. Gardiner, ME: Tilbury House.
Cerullo, M. M., and B. Curtsinger. 2000. *Sea soup: Zooplankton*. Gardiner, ME: Tilbury House.
Island Institute. 1998. *Rim of the Gulf: Restoring estuaries in the Gulf of Maine*. Rockland, ME: Island Institute.

Index